Cutting Down: A CBT workbook for treating young people who self-harm

A quarter of adolescents engage in some form of self-harm and even experienced therapists can find working with these young people difficult. Based on Cognitive Behaviour Therapy (CBT), a highly effective method for working with emotional problems, *Cutting Down* offers a practical and accessible programme for mental health therapists from different professional backgrounds working with young people who self-harm.

The programme is comprised of four parts, each covering a specific stage of therapy, and is split into 27 short modules. Although designed to be delivered over a course of 14 sessions, the programme is presented in a way that allows the therapist to decide which combination of specific modules is chosen and how long is spent on each, based on the specific clinical needs of the person they are working with. Throughout the programme, virtual patients are used to illustrate the various exercises and strategies. Part One, *What's Going On?*, introduces self-harm and CBT and aims to develop insight into feelings, problems, goals and the concept of change. Part Two, *Feelings, Thoughts and Behaviour*, looks at working on activities, managing depression and identifying and managing negative thoughts. Part Three, *Coping Strategies*, introduces modules on problem-solving, assertiveness, mindfulness and alternatives to self-harm. Part Four, *On You Go!*, finishes the programme with a review of goals, identifying triggers and developing a 'first-aid kit' and a 'toolbox' of skills to reinforce the programme. Downloadable worksheets enhance the practicality of the text.

Designed to support clinicians working with adolescents engaging in self-harm, this unique workbook is ideal for counsellors, counselling psychologists, clinical psychologists, CBT therapists, IAPT practitioners, CAMHS mental health workers and nurse therapists as well as students and trainees.

Lucy Taylor is a consultant clinical psychologist at the National & Specialist Child and Adolescent Dialectical Behaviour Therapy (DBT) Service, Michael Rutter Centre for Children and Young People, South London and Maudsley, NHS Foundation Trust. She is BABCP accredited and has a private practice based in Surrey.

Mima Simic is Joint Head of the Child and Adolescent Eating Disorder Service and a consultant child and adolescent psychiatrist for the Child and Adolescent Dialectical Behaviour Therapy Service at the Michael Rutter Centre for Children and Young People, South London and Maudsley, NHS Foundation Trust.

Ulrike Schmidt is Professor of Eating Disorders at the Institute of Psychiatry, Kings College London and Honorary Consultant Psychiatrist in the Eating Disorders Unit, South London and Maudsley, NHS Foundation Trust.

Cutting Down

- A CBT workbook for treating young people who self-harm

Lucy Taylor, Mima Simic and Ulrike Schmidt

Routledge
Taylor & Francis Group

LONDON AND NEW YORK

First published 2015
by Routledge
27 Church Road, Hove, East Sussex, BN3 2FA

and by Routledge
711 Third Avenue, New York, NY 10017

Routledge is an imprint of the Taylor & Francis Group, an informa business

British Library Cataloguing in Publication Data
A catalogue record for this book is available from the British Library

Library of Congress Cataloging in Publication Data
Taylor, Lucy (Lucy M. W.)
  Cutting down : a CBT workbook for treating young people who self-harm / Lucy Taylor, Mima Simic, and Ulrike Schmidt.
    pages cm
  Includes bibliographical references and index.
  1. Self-mutilation in adolescence. 2. Adolescent psychology.
  3. Child psychology. 4. Self-destructive behavior in children
  I. Simic, Mima (Psychiatrist) II. Schmidt, Ulrike. III. Title.
  RJ506.S44T39 2015
  616.85'8200835—dc23   2014034738

ISBN: 978-0-415-62452-7 (hbk)
ISBN: 978-0-415-62453-4 (pbk)
ISBN: 978-1-315-81797-2 (ebk)

Typeset in Stone Serif
by Keystroke, Station Road, Codsall, Wolverhampton

Contents

CONTENTS

Acknowledgements

I would like to thank all those staff and clients who contributed to the pilot of the manual. Many thanks to Professor Kate Davidson, Ms Clair Richards and Ms Anna Oldershaw for their hard work and input into the original manual. I offer my thanks to assistant psychologists Rosalind Payne and Lisa Goodwin for their invaluable help with putting the worksheets and pictures together and giving feedback and technological help with the manuscript.

I would also like to acknowledge the specialists in the field to whom I have referred throughout the book – in particular Marsha Linehan.

I offer special thanks to the young people who have worked hard to illustrate the concepts and add their creativity and input to the book.

Lucy M.W. Taylor
London 2013

Acknowledgements

Introduction to the programme

Who the programme is for and how to use it

This book is designed for mental health therapists working with young people who self-harm. The content was originally designed for one-to-one use, but the materials could translate to a group context as the skills are generic to common maintenance factors in self-harm. For the purposes of this treatment programme, self-harm is defined as 'causing deliberate hurt to your own body'. From the statistics, we know that up to a quarter of all adolescents engage in self-harm behaviour each year, with indications from the literature that this has increased over time. A recent piece of research carried out by Young Minds stated that self-harm inpatient admissions had increased by 68 per cent over the last ten years.(1) The need for effective treatments for young people who self-harm is evident.

This book uses evidence-based strategies, in particular Cognitive Behaviour Therapy (CBT), and is based on a flexible and formulation-driven model. The assessment and treatment techniques in this book have been effective with young people who self-harm but who do not meet criteria for diagnosis of an emerging personality disorder and do not feel regularly suicidal. It is particularly suited to younger adolescents, and young people with symptoms of depression and/or anxiety. The book takes on a CBT approach and focuses on maintaining factors to self-harm. Although there are some 'acceptance' strategies similar to those used within Dialectical Behaviour Therapy (DBT), the main aim of the book is to help the young person understand the factors that serve to maintain their problems and to teach them adaptive skills to address emotional difficulties. We know that the most common methods of self-harm in young people are cutting and taking overdoses, but this programme is designed to treat a whole range of self-harm behaviours. Feedback from therapists and young people who have used the manual has been positive. Therapists have reported that they like the 'session-by-session' structure and have found the book particularly useful, as it addresses the majority of problems traditionally associated with self-harm: for example, low mood, anxiety, anger, lack of assertiveness and difficulties with problem-solving. In other words, it has a trans-diagnostic flavour which lends itself well to individual formulations and tailored treatment. The young people themselves reported that they liked the idea of virtual clients. They were able to relate to some shared issues and found it useful to observe other like-minded young people 'bringing' their own problems to the session and specific treatment strategies being illustrated.

Essential elements for the development of the *Cutting Down* programme have been identified through a comprehensive review of the evidence base on treatment of self-harm and associated psychological maintenance factors. Depression and anxiety have been shown to be common co-morbid factors linked with self-harm and thus the appropriate treatments for these conditions have been incorporated in the programme.

The book is comprised of four parts: 'What's going on?'; 'Feelings, thoughts and behaviour (FTB)'; 'Coping strategies'; and 'On you go!' Each part covers specific stages of therapy. The parts are divided into a number of modules that address specific interventions or skills. The programme is designed to be delivered in fourteen sessions; however, the expectation is that the therapist, together with the young person, will decide which combination of specific modules is chosen and/or the length of time spent on each module. This will be based on the specific clinical needs of the young person. In addition, fifty-one worksheets are included in a separate section at the end of the book – these can be downloaded free of charge by purchasers of the printed version, and are used as working material for specific sessions or homework between sessions. The worksheets are designed to be used in line with the book. Modules are presented in a particular order; however, the order of the modules in the 'Coping strategies' part of the workbook can be more flexible, again based on the specific needs of the young person. It is recommended that the reader look through the whole book prior to starting therapy with a young person. This will help the therapist decide whether it may be useful to offer some coping strategies at the beginning or early on in treatment. This can help to keep the young person motivated and to start managing self-harm immediately and safely.

There are homework exercises for the young person to complete between sessions.

Initial modules focus on psycho-education and a comprehensive cognitive behavioural assessment of the self-harm behaviour. Levels of motivation for giving up/reducing self-harm are assessed using simple 'motivational rulers' adapted from Rollnick and Millers' work.(2) If motivation is assessed to be low, adolescents are encouraged to weigh up the 'costs' and 'benefits' of their self-harm and related problematic behaviours, and to challenge their current beliefs about the utility of self-harm in their life.

The programme introduces 'virtual patients' with their own stories of self-harm: Jessica, Cassie, Mark and Katy. These characters are used as illustrative examples throughout, to demonstrate how they have coped with particular problems that led to self-harm (e.g. lack of assertiveness or self-critical thoughts). Download Worksheet 1: Real-life stories, for a snapshot of their stories.

General issues to consider during therapy

The terms 'feelings' and 'emotions' are used interchangeably through the book as meaning the same thing – technically, emotions. Young people have reported to us that they often prefer the term 'feelings'. However, it is important to bear in mind that clinical experience has shown that people can easily mix up thoughts and feelings. As it is very important in CBT to become adept at recognising the difference between a thought and a feeling, consideration of terminology and each young person's understanding of thoughts and feelings throughout the book is recommended. A key aspect of the treatment throughout will be helping the young person distinguish thoughts from emotions on a daily basis.

The therapeutic alliance

From discussions with young people in therapy, we know that some aspects of building a therapeutic alliance are particularly difficult for them, namely:

Trust

Being able to trust a therapist can be extremely troublesome for young people. As a therapist, you cannot force someone to trust you. However, there are things you can do to help the trust-building process:

- Always be open with clients about confidentiality and serious risk situations, when some information might be shared with others. Explain that in any of these instances, sharing of information will be discussed first with the young person and they will know in advance what is shared, and with whom.
- Introduce the issue of trust into a session very early on. Have an open conversation with the young person about trust and show that you recognise that trust can be difficult, and take time to achieve. You could tie this in with talking about the collaborative nature of CBT. Explain that trust works in both directions and that during the course of therapy you will both need to try to build trust with one another. Make it clear that, whenever the young person feels trust is an issue throughout the course of therapy, they should be open about this.

Making connections

Young people can sometimes feel that they don't connect with their therapist. This can make them feel that the therapist doesn't really understand them and the way they feel. As a therapist, you will also find that you connect more easily with some young people than others.

Trying to engage the young person by being as active as possible in therapy may help to establish a better connection. Also, make them feel heard by reflecting back to them regularly, listening carefully to what they are saying, and getting feedback from them at the end of sessions. As much as possible, show that you have actively done something to respond to any feedback you receive.

General things to remember throughout therapy

- Set an agenda at the start of each session. Although this book is fairly prescriptive, and there are specific issues to cover per session, it is also important to ask the young person what they want to bring to the session. The young person will be less likely to attend to the information during the session if they are preoccupied with their own problems. Try to get into the habit of agreeing a joint agenda. This will include: review of homework from the previous week; bridge from the last session (to ensure that everything previously covered has been understood and remembered); your plan for the session; and some time for an agenda item the young person has brought. Timing the agenda items is very important, to enable the bulk of time to be spent on the new topic for the week. Whilst setting the agenda, agree with the young person how much time you will spend on each issue. A guide to this timing might be: five-minute catch-up and agenda-setting; five-minute bridge from last session; ten to fifteen minutes for the young person's topic (unnecessary if the young person does not have anything specific he/she wants to discuss); twenty-five to thirty minutes for the specific session's topic; and ten minutes for feedback and homework-setting. Some of the homework-setting will happen during the session topic but it is useful to recap with the young person what they are planning to carry out at home at the end of the session.
- The book is not intended to be rigid in its approach: timings are flexible, and it is important to remember that in all cases clinical judgement prevails, in particular when taking time out of the session structure to discuss and assess immediate risk issues. Similarly, if a young person brings a crisis to the session that they want to talk about, then it may be appropriate to devote some time to this away from the book plan. However, as much as possible, try to link it into the work you are doing, and draw on their crisis as an example to reinforce an idea or introduce a future coping or problem-solving technique.

Formulation

The book emphasises work on formulation from the start. Psychological formulation is viewed as a shared narrative, or a story that is constructed throughout the course of assessment and treatment and draws on the young person's personal meaning attributed to their life experiences. The task of the CBT therapist in constructing a useful formulation is to use their clinical skills to combine psychological theory/principles/evidence with personal thoughts, feelings and meanings. This is done through 'a process of ongoing collaborative sense-making'(3) in order to develop a shared account that indicates the most helpful way forward. Although the therapy model of this book is rooted in Beck's Cognitive Model,(4) it also draws on Gillian Butler's work (5) in aiming to construct a 'plausible account' of the young person's experiences. Due to the nature of the young person's problems, the book also takes a trans-diagnostic approach within CBT: in other words, a form of CBT that targets cognitive and behavioural processes common to a range of mood disorders.

Start work on developing your formulation as soon as possible. As a therapist, it is a good idea to jot down information you have from the point of referral, continuing through the assessment and into the treatment sessions. Use the formulation sheet 'My journey', worksheet 33, from Part Two, to jot ideas down by yourself, in the first instance, prior to the allocated collaborative formulation section later in the book. You will find a time when it feels clinically appropriate to start to share the formulation with the young person, but use the workbook's timing as a useful guide.

End of session feedback

At the end of every session, get feedback from the young person on what they have found useful and less useful from the session. It helps you to guide the next sessions and remember what is useful to the young person, whilst appreciating their individual learning style. When you ask what has been particularly difficult for the young person in the session, you might say, 'Is there anything that you found useful, difficult, rubbed you up the wrong way, did not find useful today?' or 'Was it easy/hard to talk to me about your difficulties? Is there anything I could have done to make it easier?' Suggestions for asking what they found useful might include: 'What was useful about today's session? What will you take away from today?'

Ending therapy

In Part Four, there are suggestions and tips about how to end therapy. However, planning for the end needs to start from the beginning of treatment. Some young people build fast and trusting relationships with their therapist and may have struggled with attachments in the past. As well as this, self-harm and other behaviours may have served a strong communication function for the young person and when they end a relationship, they might feel especially distressed. Some young people might have become accustomed to using self-harm as a default mechanism to manage such situations. It is important that you fully understand the functions of self-harm for the young person, so that you are aware of the behaviours and responses from others that might reinforce these behaviours. A good formulation and functional analyses of self-harm behaviours are crucial. Be mindful of your reaction to specific behaviours and the attention paid. Be clear from the outset about the boundaries of therapy, where your confidentiality boundary ends and issues that will need to be shared with parents or carers (ideally with the young person's consent or jointly with them). It is important to maintain a balance between continuing with the scheduled session structure and spending appropriate time and attention on risk assessment and crisis management. This can be more of an issue at the end of treatment (see notes on 'goodbyes' on pp. 137–138).

Measuring effectiveness

A pilot study carried out by the authors of this book with adolescents seen in a community CAMHS setting, using the book (in manual form), demonstrated significant reductions in self-harm behaviour, depression symptoms and trait anxiety after eight to twelve sessions.(6) Although the number of sessions was deemed to be too short by the therapists, the positive results led to further development of the manual and publication of this book.

It is clearly good CBT practice to measure change objectively and regularly. There are several possible options the therapist might use to measure change: the children's IAPT (Improved Access to Psychological Therapies) has published a set of measures and provided evidence that session-by-session outcomes can be extremely helpful for clients. This enables young people to see that change really is happening as well as informing the therapist if change isn't that evident. Examples of measures used in IAPT are the Revised Children's Anxiety and Depression Scale (RCADS),(7) the Strengths and Difficulties Questionnaire(8) and the Outcome Rating Scale (ORS).(9) The RCADS is a forty-seven-item youth self-report questionnaire with subscales including: separation anxiety disorder (SAD); social phobia (SP); generalised anxiety disorder (GAD); panic disorder (PD); obsessive compulsive disorder (OCD); and major depressive disorder (MDD). It also yields a Total Anxiety Scale (sum of the five anxiety subscales) and a Total Internalizing Scale (sum of all six subscales). Items are rated on a four-point Likert scale from 0 ('never') to 3 ('always'). IAPT also use session-by-session measures, for example goal tracking, where the therapist and young person use the review of goals to check progress against the agreed focus, general wellbeing tracking, which uses the ORS to track general wellbeing, and symptom tracking.

Three other suggested measures to use that can be downloaded free of charge from the internet are: the Mood and Feelings Questionnaire(10); the Rosenberg Self-esteem Scale(11); and the Screen for Child Anxiety Related Emotional Disorders (SCARED-R).(12)

Whichever measures are used, they should be administered at the beginning of therapy, mid-way (end of Part Two) and at the last session.

Table 1 Self-harm log

Date	Self-harm		
	Urge	Action/how many incidents?	What did you do?
Monday			
Tuesday			
Wednesday			
Thursday			
Friday			
Saturday			
Sunday			

Rating scale for emotions and urges: 0 = Not at all; 1 = A bit; 2 = Somewhat; 3 = Rather strong; 4 = Very strong; 5 = Extremely strong

It is also useful to measure the frequency and severity of self-harm as reduction/cessation is the ultimate aim of the book. One suggestion would be the use of a diary, or log, of self-harm. Table 1 is adapted from the DBT Diary Card(13) and enables the young person and therapist to look at the extent of self-harm behaviours every week, through both urges and specific self-harm actions.

During Session 2, Module 3 identifies the young person's problems and goals. They are asked to rate their problems in terms of Subjective Units of Distress (SUDS). This rating (out of 10) is revisited at the end of Part Two and also at the end of the treatment programme.

All good CBT involves regular supervision. This book is designed for therapists who have a good knowledge of CBT and who have access to supportive CBT supervision.

References

1. Chris Lehman (2011) News article. December. www.youngminds.org.uk.
2. Rollnick, S. and Miller, W.R. (1995) What is motivational interviewing? *Behavioural and Cognitive Psychotherapy* 23, 325–334.
3. Harper, D. and Moss, D. (2003) A different kind of chemistry? Reformulating 'formulation'. *Clinical Psychology* 25, 6–10.
4. Beck, A.T. (1967) *Depression: Clinical, Experimental, and Theoretical Aspects*. New York: Harper & Row; Beck, A.T., Rush, A.J., Shaw, B.F. and Emery, G. (1979) *Cognitive Therapy of Depression*. New York: Guilford Publications.
5. Butler, G., Fennell, M. and Hackmann, A. (2008) *Cognitive-Behavioral Therapy for Anxiety Disorders: Mastering Clinical Challenges*. New York: Guilford Press.

6. Taylor, L.M.W., Oldershaw, A., Richards, C., Davidson, K., Schmidt, U. and Simic, M. (2011) Development and pilot evaluation of a manualized cognitive-behavioural treatment package for adolescent self-harm. *Behavioural and Cognitive Psychotherapy* 39(5), 619–625.

7. Chorpita, B.F., Yim, L.M., Moffitt, C.E., Umemoto L.A. and Francis, S.E. (2000) Assessment of symptoms of DSM-IV anxiety and depression in children: a revised Child Anxiety and Depression Scale. *Behaviour, Research and Therapy* 38, 835–855.

8. Goodman, R. (1997) The Strengths and Difficulties Questionnaire: a research note. *Journal of Child Psychology and Psychiatry* 38, 581–586.

9. Miller, S.D., Duncan, B.L., Brown, J., Sparks, J.A. and Claud, D.A. (2003) The Outcome Rating Scale: a preliminary study of the reliability, validity, and feasibility of a brief visual analog measure. *Journal of Brief Therapy* 2(2), 139–143.

10. Costello, E.J. and Angold, A. (1988) Scales to assess child and adolescent depression: checklists, screens, and nets. *Journal of the American Academy of Child and Adolescent Psychiatry* 27, 726–737.

11. Rosenberg, M. (1965) *Society and the Adolescent Self-image.* Princeton, NJ: Princeton University Press.

12. Muris, P., Merckelbach, H., Gadet, B., Moulaert, W. and Tierney S. (1999) Sensitivity for treatment effects of the screen for child anxiety related emotional disorders. *Journal of Psychopathology and Behavioral Assessment* 21(4), 323–335.

13. Miller, A.L., Rathus J.H. and Linehan, M.L. (2006) *Dialectical Behavior Therapy for Suicidal Adolescents.* New York: Guilford Publications.

What's going on?

Assessment and psycho-education

There are seven modules in the first stage of treatment which can usually be delivered in three sessions (two modules per session).

Aims of Part One

Session 1

- To educate the young person about self-harm (Module 1: What is self-harm?).
- To gain an understanding of the function of self-harm and a time-line of self-harm behaviours (Module 2: The function of self-harm).

Session 2

- To identify specific problems and goals for therapy (Module 3: Problems and goals).
- To introduce CBT and think about how this model might be useful in addressing self-harm (Module 4: What is CBT and how does it relate to my self-harm?).
- To enable the young person to identify and understand their emotions (Module 5: Getting to know your feelings).

Session 3

- To understand how self-harm fits into the young person's life (Module 6: Relationships and strengths).
- To enable the young person to be motivated to change (Module 7: Are you ready to make some changes?).

Session 1

This session covers both psycho-education and assessment. It is divided into two modules: (1) What is self-harm? and (2) The function of self-harm.

Session 1: Cribsheet for the therapist

- What is self-harm?
- The function of self-harm.
- Reasons why people self-harm.
- Time-line of self-harm.

Module 1: What is self-harm?

Aims

This module focuses on psycho-education about self-harm, alerting the young person to the fact that there are others who self-harm and that it is a topic that has been fairly well researched. During this session, therapists will share with the young person a summary of pertinent data from important research studies. Psycho-education is aimed to help young people feel less isolated and different, and to understand the mechanisms and function of behaviours.

Agenda

As this is the first session, the young person will probably not know what to expect. Explain that you will be setting an agenda for each session which will always include:

1. Bridge from last session.
2. Homework review.
3. Any issues brought from the young person (see earlier notes on this).

4. Main session topic.
5. Homework plan.
6. Feedback.

Main session topic

Today you will be discussing self-harm in general. Discuss the following issues and think with the young person how specific issues relate to their experience of self-harm:

1. Self-harm has been defined as 'causing deliberate hurt to your own body'. It is something that a person does to himself/herself on purpose that injures or damages their body. Reasons for why people do this vary.
2. Self-harm is often an expression of distress. It may or may not be because the person wants to die.
3. Self-harm can take many forms, but the most common methods are self-cutting and self-poisoning by taking an overdose of medicines. Other methods of self-harm include:

   - burning;
   - scratching;
   - hitting;
   - pulling out hair; and
   - not letting old wounds heal.

4. Anyone can self-harm, and it is more common than people think, particularly among young people in the UK.
5. People have different feelings related to self-harm, but something that many people who hurt themselves have in common are feelings of depression, loneliness and isolation and a sense that nobody understands. Another common theme is feeling desperate or overwhelmed by problems in relationships with important people in their life and thinking that there is no way out. Others feel angry and upset.
6. Some people report that during the act of self-harm, they can feel numb, relief, distracted with the physical sensations, or just a sense of being 'alive'. After self-harming, people may experience a mixture of thoughts and emotions. Some may feel extremely shaken up, or tired; others may feel nothing or in part feel pleased or relieved. Some describe feeling happy for a short time; others feel ashamed or guilty; and others just don't want to think or talk about it at all.

Module 2: The function of self-harm

Aims

This module continues with psycho-education about self-harm and also starts to elicit the particular functions of self-harm for the young person.

Start by discussing some of the documented reasons young people have given for using self-harm and ask the young person which they relate to and what other reasons of their own they might add to the list. Remember, the list is not exhaustive.

Reasons why people might self-harm

- Self-harm can be about reducing tension.
- Self-harm can be triggered by feeling hopeless; feeling that the harder you try, the more difficult things become ('like going up a down escalator').
- Self-harm may be a way to feel something real (even if that feeling is pain).
- Self-harm can provide a relief from thinking or feeling.
- Self-harm can be about wanting to die.
- Self-harm can be a response to sudden mood changes. When your mood suddenly changes and how you feel is far from the way you want to feel, then you might self-harm.
- Self-harm can be a way to gain control over life ('pulling an emergency brake on a runaway train').
- Self-harm can be an expression of anger.
- Self-harm can be a way of managing the difficult emotions someone has after being hurt or abused.
- Self-harm can be a way to make a body less attractive or allow greater ownership of your own body.
- Self-harm can be a way to punish yourself or other people.
- Self-harm can be an expression of guilt.
- Self-harm can be an act of cleansing ('it gets rid of the dirty blood').
- Self-harm can help people to cope with emotional and psychological pain.
- Self-harm can also have a calming effect. Some young people feel soothed by the sight of their own blood or by caring for their own wounds.
- Self-harm can occasionally be carried out to make a statement, or to get a response from others; it can communicate needs and emotions.

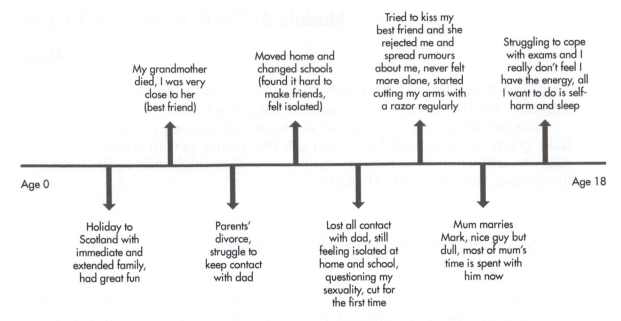

Figure 1 Time-line of self-harm: Jessica

Following this discussion, you should have a few clues as to some of the reasons why the young person engages in self-harm. The next step is to get an understanding of when the self-harm started, the triggers and frequency of occurrence. This information is gathered before carrying out a detailed functional analysis of a specific incident of self-harm. Functional analysis is important to understand what is going on for the adolescent, as well as to gather information to enable you to start the formulation of their problems. The information is used to identify the most effective treatment plan and combination of modules that you will use in treatment with this adolescent. You are trying to figure out why the young person is using self-harm as a coping strategy and what purpose it serves for them.

Exercise: Time-line of self-harm

Download Worksheet 2: Time-line of self-harm and explain that the aim of this exercise is to think about how self-harm has fitted into the young person's life and for how long. You will focus on the history, severity and frequency of self-harm. Discuss Jessica's example (Figure 1) prior to carrying out the exercise.

- First, the young person will need to identify several 'anchor points' to help remember where and why self-harm occurred: for example, key events like birthdays, special occasions, school changes, etc. These are then written/drawn around the time-line using arrows, etc.
- Next, other incidents can be added around the time-line, generated by a series of questions. 'What's your earliest memory?' 'Describe any

big event that pops into your head.' 'What is your happiest/saddest/ most exciting memory?', etc.

- Then, maybe in a different colour, incidents of self-harm can be added, again generated by a series of questions. 'Do you remember when it started?' 'When was the worst time/the most worrying time for others/the most worrying time for you?', etc.
- Then the discussion should be opened out and a chronology of incidents identified. 'Has the self-harm changed over time?' 'Have you developed routines?' 'Do you do different things now?'
- As the time-line is being completed, start to explore with the young person which particular events were happening around the various incidents/times when they self-harmed. This data will be used for the formulation and will reveal clues to predisposing, precipitating and maintaining factors.

Exercise: Functional analysis

The next exercise involves the functional analysis of a specific incident of self-harm. It might be an example from the time-line or another example that is fresh in the young person's mind. Explain that functional analysis of self-harm involves identifying the specific factors (events, emotions and thoughts) that come before, during and after an incident of self-harm.

- Go through the following example of how one of the 'virtual clients' – Cassie – felt before, during and after an episode of self-harm. Then go on to discuss one of the young person's own incidents of self-harm.

WHY CASSIE SELF-HARMED

How Cassie felt before self-harm

What happened?
I was in my bedroom and I cut the top of my leg with a razor.

What led you to do it?
My friend said she was going to come round and help me with my homework. But she never came and when I spoke to her on the phone she wasn't even sorry. I'm sure she doesn't like me any more.

What did you feel before?
I'd got really wound up when she hadn't come, as I was worried about her. Then I felt really upset and horrible and unloved. I felt really alone.

continued

What else was important at the time (events, thoughts, memories, exhaustion, voices, etc.)?
I thought about how everyone always lets me down – my dad, my friends, my mum.

Was there anything else in the background (something current or an echo from the past)?
I know that when I cut I can feel real. I matter.

Did you spend a long time thinking about harming or was it spur of the moment, or both?
I just knew it was what I wanted to do but I couldn't straight away as I was looking after my sister. Thinking about it made me feel better.

Is that your usual way? (If not, what was the difference?)
Most of the time I generally have to wait until I'm on my own, which can be hard.

How Cassie felt after self-harm

How did you feel immediately afterwards?
I felt better . . . I felt a release of all that tension.

How did you feel a bit later?
The better feeling didn't last very long. I felt guilty that I had been angry with my friend and I was really worried about my mum realising what I'd done.

How do you feel about it now?
That I'm really selfish for doing it. When my mum asked me about it, I felt so ashamed . . . I knew I'd really let her down.

How do you think your self-harm has helped?
It gives me strength, it takes away the bad feeling for a while . . . and it reminds me who I am and that I matter.

How do you think it *doesn't* help?
When my mum finds out about it, she blames herself and gets all upset and that just kills me. I end up hating myself even more, which makes me feel even worse.

Is there anything you would have done differently?
I can't think of anything. I'm so useless.

Is that your usual way? (If not, what was the difference?)
Pretty much . . . but sometimes I cut my arms or stomach. It depends.

How do you feel now?
Really just horrible! I'm stupid and selfish. I feel guilty and sore.

Next download Worksheet 3: Why you self-harmed, and go through a recent incident of self-harm that the young person can remember clearly. Use prompts to get as much detailed information as possible. 'Who was around?' 'Where were you?' 'Can you remember what you could see/smell, etc.?' Use this information to complete the worksheet together.

Explain to the young person that this information will be really useful to start to understand the role of thoughts, emotions and behaviour in self-harm. It will also be useful in thinking about the therapy path and the young person's goals for recovery, which will be addressed in the next session.

End of Session 1

- At this stage it might be useful to introduce Module 23: Alternatives to self-harm, so that the young person can start to think about testing out different behaviours to try to reduce the self-harm from the start. You will need to make a clinical judgement as to whether this would be a good idea so early on. The benefit is that the young person feels they have some choices and often feels very motivated to try new ideas. You can use feedback from them as to when alternatives worked and when they didn't.
- Homework: complete a functional analysis of an incident of self-harm during the week on their own.
- Feedback from session.

HANDOUT FOR THE YOUNG PERSON: SESSION 1

Reasons why people might self-harm

- Self-harm can be about reducing tension.
- Self-harm can be triggered by feeling hopeless; feeling that the harder you try, the more difficult things become ('like going up a down escalator').
- Self-harm may be a way to feel something real (even if that feeling is pain).
- Self-harm can provide a relief from thinking or feeling.
- Self-harm can be about wanting to die.
- Self-harm can be a response to sudden mood changes. When your mood suddenly changes and how you feel is far from the way you want to feel, then you might self-harm.
- Self-harm can be a way to gain control over life ('pulling an emergency brake on a runaway train').
- Self-harm can be an expression of anger.
- Self-harm can be a way of managing the difficult emotions someone has after being hurt or abused.
- Self-harm can be a way to make a body less attractive or allow greater ownership of your own body.
- Self-harm can be a way to punish yourself or other people.
- Self-harm can be an expression of guilt.
- Self-harm can be an act of cleansing ('it gets rid of the dirty blood').
- Self-harm can help people to cope with emotional and psychological pain.
- Self-harm can also have a calming effect. Some young people feel soothed by the sight of their own blood or by caring for their own wounds.
- Self-harm can occasionally be carried out to make a statement, or to get a response from others; it can communicate needs and emotions.

Useful information about self-harm (from www.self-harm. co.uk)

It is almost impossible to say how many young people are self-harming. This is because very few teenagers tell anyone what's going on, so it's incredibly difficult to keep records or have an accurate idea of how many people are struggling. It is thought that around 10 per cent of young people may try to hurt themselves on purpose at some point, but the figure could be much higher. Around 90 per cent of young people treated for self-harm in A&E departments will have taken an overdose, yet the preferred method of self-harm is to cut. This means that a great many young people who are struggling with self-harm have not yet come to the attention of health services.

Session 2

Session 2 is comprised of three modules (3, 4 and 5). We start by identifying the young person's problems and the specific goals they want to achieve in therapy. After this, we introduce the CBT model and describe how it can be used to help them achieve their identified goals. Finally, in this session, the first key aspect of CBT – 'feelings' – is introduced. (As was explained in the Introduction, the terms 'feelings' and 'emotions' are used interchangeably throughout the book to mean the same thing – technically, emotions.)

Session 2: Cribsheet for the therapist

- Identifying problems and goals.
- What is CBT?
- What are emotions?
- Keeping a feelings diary.

The sessions follow the same structure throughout the treatment; each starts with an agenda.

Agenda

1. Bridge from last session (e.g. 'What do you remember from our last session?'). You might want to go through the Session 1 sheets briefly with the young person.
2. Homework review. How it went, any problems, what they learned from it and how we might build on it. What is the next step to generalise the learning? Remember to ask how the young person got on with trying the 'alternatives to self-harm', if you discussed this as a plan last week.
3. Any issues raised by the young person (see notes on this in the Introduction).
4. Main session topic.
5. Homework plan.
6. Feedback.

Module 3: Problems and goals

Aims

The aim of this module is to get a full understanding of the young person's current difficulties and definition of problems, how severe they are and to identify the specific goals they want to achieve in therapy.

Using Worksheet 4: Problems and goals, and the key points listed below, draw up an agreed problem list and ask the young person to rate how bad it is now on a personal scale of 1–10 (10 = worst, 1 = best).

Key points:

- What areas are causing problems in the young person's life?
- Define the problems clearly and specifically.
- Break down vague goals into behavioural and measurable concepts. They must be realistic and clearly defined, so that it is clear when they are achieved. For example, if the young person says, 'I want to feel better', ask them, 'How would you and/or others know you were feeling better about yourself?' and 'What would you be doing differently if you felt better?'

KATY'S PROBLEMS

Problem	Rating
1. Difficulty getting on with my mum	9
2. Feeling bad about myself	8
3. Cutting my arms	8
4. Not being able to say what I think	5

Note that young people sometimes believe there is a great discrepancy between how they feel compared with how they would like to feel, or where they would like to be. This can often lead to a sense of hopelessness (which in turn may contribute to an episode of self-harm). When discussing goal-setting, recognise this difference and try to introduce a sense of hope that realistic achievements and changes can occur by working together and by learning the CBT strategies.

KATY'S GOALS

- Fewer arguments with Mum; more 'fun' time with her. Talk to each other more (calmly).
- Increased confidence (saying what I want more to my friends, making decisions myself, not worrying about asking teachers for help), going back to trying to look good, e.g. putting on make-up, nail varnish, etc., and taking care of my appearance.

- Stop cutting – find different ways to manage my feelings.
- Learn to stick up for myself and say what I think. I need to believe that I have a valid opinion and that it matters as much as other people's.

Module 4: What is CBT and how does it relate to my self-harm?

Aim

This module aims to educate the young person about the main principles of CBT and how this way of working might help them reach their goals. It also links the functional analysis of their self-harm, as discussed in Session 1, to CBT by highlighting the relationship between thoughts, emotions, behaviours and environmental factors. It aims to educate the young person in the principles of CBT and how it is useful in recognising triggers and maintenance factors in their self-harm behaviours. This will lead on to strategies to monitor and challenge thoughts directed to self-harm and learning alternative behaviours to manage intense emotions that have historically led to self-harm.

Start by going through the young person's functional analysis and talking about the differences between thoughts, emotions and behaviours and how they are interlinked. At this point, it might be useful to discuss this more generally and educate the young person about the CBT model.

Exercise: Two scenarios

Download Worksheet 5: What is CBT? and discuss the following example with the young person

Imagine that you are at home alone (others in the house have popped out for a while) and you are sitting downstairs when you hear a loud bang upstairs (see Figure 2). Take the young person through the two possible scenarios, and encourage them to think specifically about the differences between them.

Explain to the young person that in both Scenario 1 and Scenario 2 the situation is exactly the same, but the emotions/feelings experienced vary depending on how the noise is interpreted. Ask them to write down, in their own words, the connection between thoughts and emotions and to generate examples of their own when they have noticed feeling strong emotions about something (a happy time or a time when they felt very angry). Then ask them to identify the associated thoughts and behaviours. Use Worksheet 6: The help triangle to record the various examples.

Explain that in CBT they will be learning ways to manage difficult emotions by becoming expert at identifying their thoughts. When they can do this, they will learn ways to challenge distorted thinking (thinking bias), find alternative, more adaptive ways of thinking and in turn alter what they do in response to the thoughts.

21

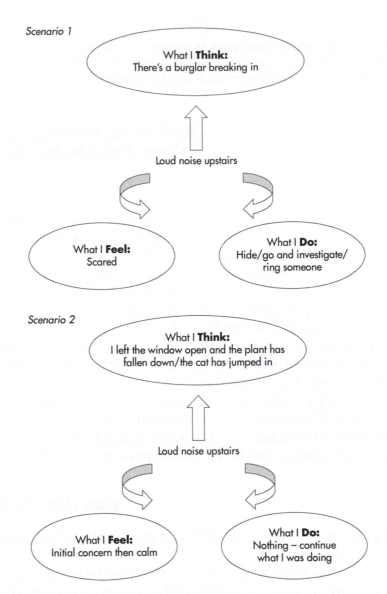

Scenario 1

What I **Think:**
There's a burglar breaking in

Loud noise upstairs

What I **Feel:**
Scared

What I **Do:**
Hide/go and investigate/
ring someone

Scenario 2

What I **Think:**
I left the window open and the plant has
fallen down/the cat has jumped in

Loud noise upstairs

What I **Feel:**
Initial concern then calm

What I **Do:**
Nothing – continue
what I was doing

Figure 2 Two scenarios

Module 5: Getting to know your feelings

Aims

This module continues to focus on aspects of CBT and aims to address
the next key aspect of CBT – feelings/emotions. The idea is to help the
young person be more tuned into how they are feeling and enable them
to increase their understanding and ability to describe their emotions.
They will learn to identify the thoughts associated with intense emotions
and in turn will be taught ways to manage and regulate their emotions.
Some of the ideas and strategies are taken and adapted from Linehan's
work on regulating emotions.(1)

Start by talking about the first step in regulating emotions: namely,
being able to identify and label current emotions. Emotions can be useful,

destructive or (rarely) neutral. As well as this, the appraisal and inter-pretation of one's own emotions influence how they are experienced. Continue with the following psycho-education on emotions.

Psycho-education

What are emotions?

The feeling of an emotion is a bit like someone knocking on your door to deliver a message. If the message is urgent, the knock is loud; if it's very urgent, the knock is very loud. If it is very urgent and you don't answer the door, the knock grows louder and louder until you either open the door or it is broken down. Whichever, the emotion will continue to bang away until it is acknowledged. As soon as you 'open the door' by listen-ing to the message, the emotion can be dealt with and it will eventually disappear.(2)

Explain to the young person that they may not experience it like this at the time: they may just want to get rid of the emotion as quickly as possible. At times, self-harm may seem like the only option when emotions are felt very strongly.

People often struggle to know which specific emotion they are feeling. As well as this, emotions are often experienced in pairs or groups, and they can feel very mixed up. Discuss the analogy of emotions mixing together like squash and water, which makes it difficult to tease them apart and name them separately. If this happens, it can feel very overwhelming for the young person.

The following exercises aim to teach the young person about different emotions, how to separate them from each other, and how to make them easier to understand and deal with.

Exercise: Different emotions

Download Worksheet 7: Unmixing the feeling cocktail. This exercise is designed to help the young person identify, decipher, understand and describe their various emotions. In addition, it helps them identify links between their emotions and their behaviour.

Tell the young person that we are going to look at their feelings in more detail. First they should look at the list of feelings in Table 2 (Worksheet 8: Emotions list).

Ask the young person to pick three of the emotions from the list. Depending on the client, you could use one of several different methods, depending on their level of emotional literacy and what they prefer:

- Close your eyes and randomly select three different emotions.
- Pick out the three emotions you most identify with.
- Pick out the three emotions you least identify with.

Table 2 Emotions

Scared	Afraid	Confident
Brave	Happy	Content
Lonely	Tearful	Calm
Hurt	Anxious	Disgusted
Disgusting	Out of control	Relaxed
Jealous	Proud	Ashamed
Embarrassed	Frustrated	Miserable
Disappointed	Helpless	Exploited
Furious	Uncomfortable	Love
Sad	Guilty	Excited
Worried	Bored	Annoyed
Used	Grumpy	Mad
Upset		

- Pick out the three emotions that other people tell you they think you exhibit.

Once they have picked their three emotions, ask them to read each one aloud and describe what it means as best as they can. You could relate this to how the young person thinks other people feel when they experience the emotion, if this is easier. Make it clear that this is not a test: some emotions are hard to describe. The idea is to try to get an impression of how the young person understands emotions and their emotional vocabulary.

Following this, introduce the feelings scale (see below and also download the picture version, Worksheet 9: Feelings scale) and encourage the young person to rate how intensely they feel certain emotions (10 = most intense; 0 = no intensity). This subjective scale will be referred to throughout the book.

Feelings scale

0	**1**	**2**	**3**	**4**	**5**	**6**	**7**	**8**	**9**	**10**
No intensity		A little feeling			Medium level of intensity			The most intense feeling		

Next, show the young person Cassie's example (see below). Then ask them the following questions about the first of the three emotions they chose earlier:

- Can you give an example of when you have recently felt like that or when you have observed a friend or relation feel like that?
- Can you describe exactly what was happening? (Help them make the link between their emotions and their behaviour.)
- Can you remember what you were thinking at the time?

CASSIE'S EXAMPLE

Cassie often feels numb inside, which is when she cuts. She recognises the following emotion that she feels she struggles to tolerate.

Scared: When your heart races so fast you think you're going to die and something horrifying is about to happen. The last time I felt like this was when I had to go to my therapy group. I thought I would be judged and everyone would hate me. Then I felt even more scared and anxious. I think that if another person my age felt scared, they would also feel the physical sensations and might avoid doing the thing that scared them.

Next, ask the young person to describe their personal experience of the other two emotions in the same way. Then ask them to try to describe how another young person of the same age might behave, and what they might be thinking if they felt like this. This gives the young person (and the therapist) an opportunity to compare their own thoughts and behaviour during certain emotional states with what they consider the norm for the particular developmental stage and the behaviours that increase the emotion instead of helping.

If the young person appears to be very emotionally literate, then it is fine to be flexible regarding the amount of time and depth you invest in this exercise.

End of Session 2

- Homework: give the young person Worksheet 10: Emotions diary as their home task for this session. Explain that keeping a diary of your feelings can be helpful in a number of ways. By looking back at the diary, you might discover that there is a link between what you were doing and how you felt. You might also find that your feelings are stronger at certain times of day, or that they are not as frequent as you thought they were.

  Following on from this homework exercise, you can draw on their diary examples when completing Worksheet 11: Feelings are our friends and Worksheet 12: What feelings do I squash, bottle or swallow? next week.
- Feedback

How to fill in the diary sheet

The diary sheet breaks each day of the week down into one-hour boxes. In each box, write the following information:

- What you were doing and who you were with.
- How you felt and the strength of that feeling on the 0–10 feelings scale.

You do not need to write in great detail; just a word or two will do.

Table 3 Cassie's emotion diary

DAY →	MONDAY
TIME ↓	
8–9 am	Lying awake in bed SAD 9
9–10 am	Got up late for school SAD 7
10–11 am	In English lesson WORRIED 4
11–12 pm	Still in lesson WORRIED 5
12–1 pm	Lunch break alone SAD 10
1–2 pm	In PE with friends WORRIED 8
2–3 pm	In English OK 5
3–4 pm	Walk home from school OK 6
4–5 pm	Tea with mum IRRITATED 7
5–6 pm	Up in my room MISERABLE 8
6–7 pm	Talked to my sister HAPPY 6
7–8 pm	Dinner with family BORING 7

DAY →	MONDAY
TIME ↓	
8–9 pm	Watch TV RELAXED 8
9–10 pm	
10–11 pm	Went to bed WORRY 8
11–12 am	Can't sleep WORRY 10

References

1. Linehan, M. (1993) *Cognitive Behaviour Treatment of Borderline Personality Disorder*. New York: Guilford Press.
2. McKenna, P. (2007) *I Can Make You Thin*. London: Bantam Press.

HANDOUT FOR THE YOUNG PERSON: SESSION 2

Problems and goals

- You will learn how to outline your problems and define the specific goals.

What is CBT?

- CBT is about learning ways to manage difficult emotions by becoming an expert at identifying your thoughts. When you have got good at this, you will learn ways to challenge thinking biases and find alternative, more balanced ways of thinking and in turn change what you do in response to the thoughts.
- Step one is to become 'tuned in' to how you are feeling and to get good at describing your emotions. When you experience an intense feeling, it is usually linked with a thought.

Things to remember about emotions

- The feeling of an emotion is a bit like someone knocking on your door to deliver a message. If the message is urgent, the knock is loud; if it's very urgent, the knock is very loud. If it is very urgent and you don't answer the door, the knock grows louder and louder until you either open the door or it is broken down. Whichever, the emotion will continue to bang away until it is acknowledged. As soon as you 'open the door' by listening to the message, the emotion can be dealt with and it will eventually disappear. At the time, you may just want to get rid of the emotion as quickly as possible and self-harm may seem like the only option when emotions are felt very strongly.
- Emotions can be useful, problematic or (rarely) neutral. As well as this, how you interpret and understand your emotions influences how you experience them.
- Many people struggle to know which specific emotion they are feeling, and you may often experience emotions in pairs or groups, so they can feel very mixed up. This is a bit like the way squash mixes with water, which makes it difficult to tease them apart and name them separately. If this happens, you might feel overwhelmed.
- Keeping a feelings diary can be helpful in a number of ways. By looking back at the diary, you might discover that there is a link between what you were doing and how you felt. You might find that your feelings are stronger at certain times of day, or that they are not as frequent as you thought they were.

Session 3

This session starts with some exercises about emotions based on the previous homework. Following this, Modules 6 and 7 address key relationships (potential protective factors) and motivation to change.

The overall aim of this session is to continue the work from Module 5 on emotions and get some sense of the young person's life and relationships outside of therapy. This should be enhancing engagement and leading to the next part of the assessment – to understand the young person's relationships (Module 6). The session finishes with the assessment of motivation to change and, if needed, leads to further work on the young person's motivation for change (Module 7).

Session 3: Cribsheet for the therapist

- The function of emotions: feelings are our friends.
- The impact of relationships on self-harm.
- Looking at the young person's strengths.
- Motivation to give up self-harm.

Agenda

1. Bridge from last session.
2. Homework review (in main session topic).
3. Any issues raised by the young person.
4. Main session topic.
5. Homework plan.
6. Feedback.

Main session topic

Start the session by reviewing the emotions diary homework and think about the next step in understanding emotions. In order to continue the work on emotions, download Worksheet 11: Feelings are our friends and

Worksheet 12: What feelings do I squash, bottle or swallow? and work through these with the young person. First, look at Mark's examples below. Once you have completed this work, move to the next module, which focuses on the young person's relationships and personal strengths.

EMOTIONS ARE OUR FRIENDS: MARK

OK, so maybe this sounds a bit silly, but it's true! Think about it for a minute. Most people would say that happiness is a positive feeling, and that anger is a negative feeling, maybe even one that you shouldn't have at all. But we all have lots of different feelings at different times, and some of them are pretty unpleasant! It's not bad to feel angry; it's what you do with the feeling that counts.

Let us consider some of the positive aspects of a few of the more 'difficult' feelings.

Anger: can give you the strength to stand up for something

What does my anger do for me? Stops me being walked over (especially by my dad).

Envy: can help you strive for something

When has being envious helped me? When my brother started to beat me at running. That made me work harder to win.

Guilt: can help you change how you act

How has feeling guilty helped me? When I take out all my anger at my mum, I feel guilty. It's not her fault (it's my dad). I can then apologise and try to make her feel better.

Fear: can help us to protect ourselves

How has my fear helped me? Fear of dying has helped me to think about how to make my life better, so I actually want to live.

Shame: can help you to be more considerate of those you love in the future

How has it helped me to feel shame? My dad makes me feel shame about who I am, what I wear and my sexuality. I am starting to learn to stand up for myself but it helps a tiny bit to understand my dad's upbringing and how he wants to protect me from bullies.

Sadness: can help you to move on

How has my sadness helped me? I still feel sad, but I decided I could not deal with it on my own and it was too much. That's when I asked for help.

> **Disappointment: can help you to be more realistic in your expectations of others and yourself**
>
> When has my disappointment helped me? Realising that my dad isn't going to change. I can only try to see it from his point of view and stick up for my own values.

Squashed feelings

Self-harm is often considered to be a way of managing overwhelming feelings such as anger, frustration, despair or sadness. Sometimes it can feel like these intense feelings are so great that they will overflow like a volcano and this might be too much to handle. So, when we experience these feelings, we often try to find a way to manage them. We might swallow our feelings or bottle them up in order to feel in control of them and some people may harm themselves to get relief.

For some young people, it can be difficult even to know how to describe such intense feelings. By 'un-mixing the feelings cocktail' earlier on, they may feel more able to identify and understand their feelings. The next task is to help them to identify those particular feelings that they try to squash or bottle up.

> **MARK BOTTLES UP**
>
> - Anxiety (feels weak to show it).
> - Sadness (until it bursts out).
> - Envy (it eats away at me).

Figure 3 Cassie's 'bottle' of emotions

When you go through the exercises with the young person, ask them which feelings they tend to bottle up, or squash, or swallow. You can use the appropriate sheet, or all of them. It is useful to ask why they think they do this and what advantages/disadvantages they feel in using this strategy with their feelings.

Module 6: Relationships and strengths

Aim: relationships

To get an idea of the young person's support network and to identify who they can talk to and which interpersonal skills or problems they might have.

From the literature, it is clear that there are multiple risk and maintaining factors associated with self-harm in children and adolescents, in particular family factors,[1] such as difficulties in parent–child relationships, perceived low levels of parental caring and poor communication,[2] a family history of self-harm[3] and parental mental illness and substance abuse.[4] Many self-harm incidents are triggered by an argument with a parent (usually the mother).[5] The other maintaining factors in self-harm are psychological factors, for example depression, which is exacerbated by a negative self concept.[6] This module addresses the young person's strengths after deciphering information about key relationships in their life.

Start by telling the young person that they are now going to think more about the people in their life and how they might have an influence on their self-harm and emotions. Highlight an example from their diary when they have talked about their family or friends and say that now would be a useful time to map out where various people are placed in terms of importance, supportiveness and distance from the centre (themselves).

Exercise: The relationship map

Download Worksheet 13: My relationship map and ask them to place themselves in the centre of the map. Then ask them to consider who is in their life generally, and who is significant to them or plays a specific role in their life. These people – predominantly friends and family – should then be added to the map, with their position (near or far from the young person, in the centre) dictated by how important or how close they feel them to be. Sometimes, the young person will have a 'gut feeling' as to where to place the relation/friend; at other times, they may need to think carefully about where a person should go (not where they feel they should be placed).

Depending on the young person, this exercise can be done more creatively with the use of colours, buttons, stones or miniatures representing

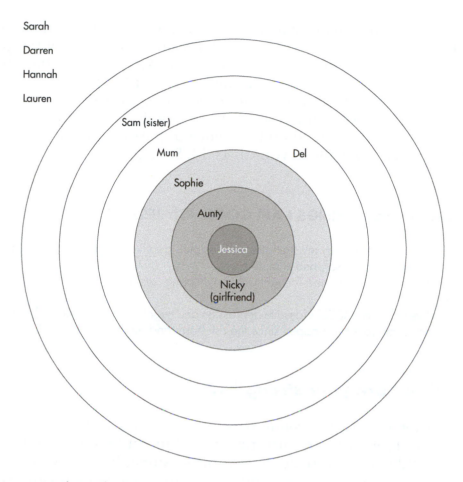

Sarah
Darren
Hannah
Lauren

Sam (sister)

Mum   Del

Sophie

Aunty

Jessica

Nicky
(girlfriend)

Figure 4 Jessica's relationship map

relationships placed on the map. You can also explore why the young person has chosen certain colours or miniatures for different people.

Discuss with them the differences between people they can talk to and people they are close to. Remember that a young person can be close to a parent, but this might be a difficult relationship and they may be unable to talk to them. Perhaps get them to complete the task twice, using different colours to plot the first group and then the second. This will highlight people who fall into both categories as they will be signified by both colours.

Explain that this exercise can also help us to think about how to use the support of those close to the young person to avoid self-harm and increase communication. This can be referred to when thinking about coping strategies later.

Aim: strengths

As we saw in Module 5, the literature indicates that repeated self-harm in adolescence is associated with a wide variety of psychological factors, such as depression, hopelessness, trait anger, lower self-esteem and poor self-rated problem-solving ability. As well as this, the young person may have become quite attached to the self-harm and if they are contemplating this being 'taken away', it is important to know what other, more functional behaviours might substitute for the self-harm.

The aim of this section is to help the young person identify their strengths. It is important that they do not feel solely defined by their self-harm and start to find evidence of positive qualities to raise their self-esteem. Download Worksheet 14: Strengths.

MY STRENGTHS – THINGS I AM GOOD AT!: JESSICA

- What would my family say my strengths are? Helpful, creative (good at writing), clever (although I don't think so), beautiful, talented.
- Why do my friends like me? Thoughtful, funny, caring, strong, approachable, loyal, bubbly.
- Things I've achieved? GCSEs (despite depression and negative teacher attitude), swimming for county (but I've stopped since the self-harm and depression started).

Exercise: What are your strengths?

For this exercise, ask the young person to think about the things they are good at. Prompt them with triggers that might help the discussion. 'What would your best friend say was nice/a strength about you?' 'Why do your friends like you as a friend?' 'Have they said what qualities you have that make you a good friend?' 'What have teachers/family said about you that is positive?' 'Have there been any times when you have achieved something/won something, etc.?' The aim of this exercise is to find evidence for various strengths to help boost the young person's self-esteem (see End of Session 3 Homework on pp. 38–39).

Module 7: Are you ready to make some changes?

Aim

This module aims to assess motivation to change, in preparation for the next phase of therapy and to find alternative ways to manage problems other than self-harm. We know from the research that the interaction between a therapist and a client powerfully influences client resistance, compliance and change.

It is not unusual for people who self-harm to feel ashamed or embarrassed about their way of coping. However, it can also be difficult for the young person to think about what their life would be like without self-harm, and they can feel ambivalent or even unmotivated to give it up. There are many reasons why they may not be able or ready to change. Even so, the fact that they are starting to engage with this programme implies that at least a small part of them (or someone who cares about them) is considering change.

Exercise: Are you ready to make changes?

Download Worksheet 15: Are you ready to make changes? to assess the young person's motivation using the simple 'motivational rulers'.(7) Then complete the questions with the young person. If motivation is assessed to be low, encourage the young person to weigh up the 'costs' and 'benefits' of their self-harm and related problematic behaviours they may have started to discuss.

Look at what Mark said when asked how useful self-harm is in his life (see box). Then ask the young person the same question and discuss.

ARE YOU READY TO MAKE CHANGES?: MARK

Mark would like to stop cutting himself but he is finding it very difficult to stop, particularly when he is feeling anxious or low. He describes how the sight of his blood helps relieve tension and induces a sense of calmness. It also makes him 'feel real'. However, Mark recognises that his self-injury provides only temporary relief and is not the solution to his problems. Furthermore, he feels guilty that his self-harming behaviour is causing more arguments between his parents and leading his mother to worry about him. Mark has stated that he would like to overcome his urges to self-harm by finding more healthy or alternative ways to deal with difficult feelings.

Tips when going through the worksheet (adapted from Bell(8)):

- Try to use open-ended questions: for example, 'Tell me about . . .'
- Validate by expressing why the young person might be experiencing something: for example, 'It's natural you should have mixed emotions.'
- Make sure you effectively listen and summarise what the young person is saying: for example, 'Is this what you mean?'
- Try to include motivational statements relating to the young person's recognition of the problem; any concerns they might have about the effects (now and in the future) on family, friends, health; their current intention to change; their level of optimism and past experience of self-efficacy (i.e. when they have successfully effected change in the past).
- Explore the young person's goals: for example, 'What is important in your life?' and 'How does your problem get in the way?'

If the scores are below 5 (but more than 2), this means that more motivational work might be useful. Explain to the young person that you will be doing some further work on motivation using more exercises and downloadable worksheets (see next section).

Exercise: Getting motivated

The aim of this exercise is to continue thinking about the young person's motivation for change. This exercise is optional and depends on the level of motivation of the young person. Looking back at their answers on Worksheet 15 will help you decide whether motivation is an issue for the young person. If they lack motivation to change or feel ambivalent about giving up self-harm, this exercise might prove useful.

Start by letting the young person know that you will be working on their reasons why they are reluctant to give up self-harm. Explain that it is very common to have mixed feelings about entering therapy to give this up, in part because it can feel like an effective short-term solution to seemingly intolerable distress. However, something has brought them to therapy, which implies a kernel of motivation or at least curiosity for change. Let them know that you are ready to work with them to make an informed choice and address any ambivalence or reluctance.

Explain that you will be exploring the pros and cons of self-harm. Download Worksheet 16: Getting things into balance and discuss with the young person the balance sheet of 'virtual client' Jessica (see box), who is fifteen and cuts herself on a regular basis.

THE PROS AND CONS OF SELF-HARM: JESSICA

Good things about my self-harm for me *now*	**Not so good things about my self-harm for me *now***
It makes me calm and focused	It makes me ashamed that I haven't been able to cope better and it hurts
I like the sight of blood	Some of the scars look ugly
It wipes away any bad feelings	

Good things about my self-harm in my relationships with other people *now*	**Not so good things about my self-harm in my relationships with other people *now***
It gets people to notice how upset I am	It doesn't solve any of my difficulties with other people
	It makes people I care about upset

Instruct the young person that they should think about the positive and negative aspects of self-harm. It might be that their family/friends have different perspectives on self-harm, so the young person should try to take a step back and look at self-harm from different angles. Ask them to:

• Identify the pros and cons of self-harm for them *now*.
• Identify the pros and cons of their self-harm in relation to other people. Does it make people angry? Does it stop people having a go at them?

- Look into the future (say three, five or ten years from now, depending on their ability to envisage this). What might the pros and cons of self-harm be at this stage in their life? It might be useful to identify a few markers, such as, 'What do you think you will be doing in five years' time? Might you be working, living with a friend, in a relationship?' This helps the young person to visualise life in the future.
- Reflect on their self-harm in relation to other people in the future: for example, 'If you are living with a friend and self-harm is still in your life when you are twenty, what might be the pros and cons?'

Exercise: Looking at self-harm through other people's eyes (role-play)

Download Worksheet 17: Looking at self-harm through other people's eyes. The aim of this exercise is to enable the young person to explore how others view their self-harm. This can be done through either role-play or letter-writing. See Cassie's example of a role-playing exercise.

ROLE-PLAY: CASSIE

Cassie and her therapist carried out a role-play so that Cassie could gain insight into herself and others. Cassie adopted the role of someone whom she respected and valued – her best friend Emma – whilst the therapist assumed the role of Cassie herself. The therapist then asked Cassie/Emma several open-ended questions:

- How do you see me? You seem happy but there are times when I know you are feeling sad and I want to be there for you.
- How has it affected you? I am concerned about you but I am often scared to raise the topic of your self-harming in case you get angry or defensive with me. When you go off by yourself, I'm always very worried about you and I would like to support you more if you would let me.
- What are your thoughts and emotions? I'm frightened for you and I worry that one day you will go too far and inflict a severe injury upon yourself or worse.
- What advice would you give me? I would advise you to call me or someone else when you are feeling low and we will try to distract you, listen to some uplifting music or watch your favourite television programmes. I would advise you to relax and focus on something pleasant. If you've already cut yourself, I would tell you not to feel ashamed or weak but to try to prevent it happening again.

In a role-play, with the therapist pretending to be the young person each time, ask the young person to adopt three different personas in turn:

- An adult figure, such as a teacher, a family friend, a favourite aunt or a parent. They should respect this person and know they will be fair. If they do not know someone like that in real life, they should invent a person with those qualities, or use a character from TV, a film or a book. Once 'in character', they should be encouraged to talk to the therapist in that person's voice about how they understand and see the young person's self-harm, including offering advice on how the young person might change their life for the better. (five minutes)

- A close and kind friend – someone who accepts the young person no matter what and whom they trust deeply. (Again, if they can't think of anyone like that, they should invent such a friend.) How does this friend see them? How has the self-harm affected them? What are their thoughts and emotions? What advice do they have for now and the future? Again, the young person should be encouraged to answer these questions 'in character', as the friend. (five minutes)
- An older and wiser version of the young person himself/herself. What would they tell their younger self? What advice would they give? (five minutes)

Spend the final five minutes thinking back over what you have discussed and ask the young person to write down what they've learned from the exercise.

Exercise: Thinking about the future

Download Worksheet 18: Thinking about the future. The aim of this exercise is to enable the young person to think about their future and the long-term impact of self-harm on their life. It is therefore another motivation exercise.

THINKING ABOUT THE FUTURE: KATY

When the therapist asked Katy to reflect on the long-term impact of her self-harming behaviour, she described how she did not want her future husband or children to see her body covered in scars. She also feared that one day she might get a serious infection, accidentally cut too deep or take too many pills. Keeping her self-harm a secret from her family resulted in feelings of shame and she often lashed out at her parents and siblings, fearing that they would discover what she was doing. As a result, Katy felt a growing separation between her and her family and she worried that she would become isolated from them in the future.

End of Session 3

- Homework: this can be from any of the modules covered and will depend on whether you are working on the motivation of the young person. If you are *not* focusing on motivation, and see this session as primarily an assessment, you could ask the young person to spend the week in self-observation to identify their strengths. Tips for this could include noting when someone gives them a compliment or asking a friend what they think they are good at. They might ask a few close friends (or family members) to each list three qualities they like about the young person and bring these to the next session. In addition, you could ask the young person to pick three strengths they have identified about themselves, and to spend the week logging examples and situations which evidence times they have demonstrated these particular strengths. If you *have* been working on motivation, set two homework assignments: the letter-writing part of Worksheet 17; and the forward thinking exercise. The latter is useful even if the young person is already motivated to give up self-harm as it can strengthen their motivation and it links with their goals. It also provides another opportunity for the young person to think about whether they are ready to change as it prompts them to consider two alternative futures: if they are still self-harming and if they no longer self-harm.

- Feedback.

References

1. Bridge, J.A., Goldstein, T.R. and Brent, D.A. (2006) Adolescent suicide and suicidal behaviour. *Journal of Child Psychology and Psychiatry* 47, 372–394.
2. Fergusson, D.M., Woodward, L. and Horwood, L.J. (2000) Risk factors and life processes associated with the onset of suicidal behaviour during adolescence and early adulthood. *Psychological Medicine* 30, 23–39.
3. Agerbo, E., Nordentoft, M. and Mortensen, P.B. (2002) Familial, psychiatric and socioeconomic risk factors for suicide in young people: a nested case control study. *British Medical Journal* 325, 74–77; Brent, D., Perper, J.A., Moritz, G. and Liotus, L. (1994) Familial risk factors for adolescent suicide: a case-controlled study. *Acta Psychiatrica Scandinavica* 89, 52–58; Hawton, K., Rodhan K., Evans E. and Weatherall R. (2002) Deliberate self-harm in adolescents: self report survey in schools in England. *British Medical Journal* 325, 1207–1211.
4. Bridge, J.A., Goldstein, T.R. and Brent, D.A. (2006) Adolescent suicide and suicidal behaviour. *Journal of Child Psychology and Psychiatry* 47, 372–394; Chitsabesan, P. and Harrington, R. (2003) Predicting repeat self-harm in children – how accurate can we expect to be? *European Child Adolescent Psychiatry* 12, 23–29.
5. Ougrin, D., Ng, A.V. and Low, J. (2008) Therapeutic assessment based on cognitive-analytic therapy for young people presenting with self-harm: pilot study. *Psychiatric Bulletin* 32, 423–426.
6. Hawton, K., Arensman, E., Townsend, E., Bremner, S., Feldman, E., Goldney, R., Gunnell, D., Hazell, P. and Van Heeringen, K. (1998) Deliberate self-harm: systematic review of efficacy, of psychosocial and pharmacological treatments in preventing repetition. *British Medical Journal* 317, 441–447.
7. Rollnick, S. and Miller, W.R. (1995) What is motivational interviewing? *Behavioural and Cognitive Psychotherapy* 23, 325–334.
8. Bell, L. (2003) *Managing Intense Emotions and Overcoming Self-destructive Habits: A Self-help Manual.* London: Routledge.

HANDOUT FOR THE YOUNG PERSON: SESSION 3

Your relationships outside of therapy are really important for recovery. As well as this, it is important to see how motivated you are to give up self-harm now.

Emotions are our friends – every emotion has a reason, sometimes for communication and sometimes to help us to make a change.

Self-harm is often considered to be a way of managing overwhelming feelings, such as anger, frustration, despair or sadness. Sometimes it can feel like these intense feelings are so great that they will overflow like a volcano and this might be too much to handle. So, when we experience these feelings, we often try to find a way to manage them. We might 'swallow' our feelings or bottle them up in order to feel in control of them and some people may harm themselves to get relief. For some young people, it can be difficult even to know how to describe such intense feelings. Think about what feelings you squash or bottle up.

The importance of relationships

We know from studies that there are many factors that make self-harm more likely in young people: for example, family problems, arguments with a parent (usually a mother) and depression. It is important to address problems in your relationships to get better, and use the support around you instead of self-harming.

Your strengths

We also know that people who self-harm regularly are more likely to feel hopeless and angry, have low self-esteem and find it difficult to solve problems. As well as this, many young people may have become quite attached to self-harm and they might worry about it being 'taken away,' with nothing to replace it. Identifying your strengths helps you to see what you can do well.

Are you ready to give up your self-harm?

It is not unusual that people who self-harm can feel ashamed or embarrassed about their way of coping. However, it can also be difficult for the young person to think about what their life would be like without self-harm and they can have mixed feelings about change, or even feel unmotivated to give up their self-harm. There are many reasons why they may not feel able or ready to change. Even so, the fact that you are starting to engage with this programme indicates that at least a small part of you is considering change. Think about the pros and cons of giving up self-harm for you.

Feelings, thoughts and behaviour

This section is divided into six modules. Depending on how easily the young person understands the concepts, each module should be covered in one or two sessions. The overall aim of this phase of treatment is to help the young person to develop a clearer understanding of CBT and the links between thoughts, feelings and behaviours, and to start to break the cycle by recognising their own unhelpful thought patterns. The focus of the next few modules is to learn strategies to challenge thoughts, to find a more balanced/helpful way of thinking and to piece together how they reached this point by developing a shared cognitive behavioural formulation of their problems. (Remember, we are using 'feelings' and 'emotions' interchangeably throughout the book.)

Aims of Part Two

Session 4

This session is divided into two parts: first, a review of the feelings diary from Module 5; and, second, if the young person is depressed (or has little activity listed in their feeling diary), the introduction of activity scheduling. If activity scheduling is not indicated (because the young person already engages in a healthy number of activities during a typical week, or because they are not depressed to the point of avoiding activity), then you can incorporate the 'help triangle' (Module 9) into this session.
   Specific aims are:

- Feelings diary review, to look at feelings the young person has identified, their intensity and frequency, and discuss. (Module 8)
- To identify links between feeling low and lack of pleasure, lack of a sense of achievement and little activity. The aim is to start to incorporate fun and achievement activities in the week by looking at what is missing in the feelings diary. (Module 8 continued)

Session 5 (or 4 continued)

- To introduce the concept of a cognitive behavioural link model, the 'help triangle'. (Module 9)
- Negative automatic thoughts (NATs) and the help triangle. (Module 10)

Session 6

- To identify thinking distortions, introduce cognitive restructuring, including thought challenging, evidence for and against thoughts and alternative ways of thinking. (Module 11)

Session 7

- To identify core beliefs and dysfunctional assumptions (rules for living). This session is used if the young person is particularly insightful about their difficulties, or if they are older, cognitively mature or very depressed. (Module 12)

Session 8

- To piece together past and present experiences, underlying beliefs and current maintaining factors, to help the young person understand their patterns of behaviour through a cognitive behavioural formulation. (Module13)

Psychological rationale for Modules 8–13

Self-harm in young people typically occurs within the context of other psychiatric problems.(1) Studies have identified that the majority of young people who take an overdose have been diagnosed with a major depressive disorder. In addition, self-harm has been associated with co-morbid anxiety.(2) The literature on self-harm also identifies associated underlying cognitive factors, including cognitive distortions, such as dichotomous (black-and-white) thinking, cognitive rigidity(3) and dysfunctional assumptions.(4) Many young people engage in repeated self-harm and this repetition in adolescence has been associated with a wide variety of other psychological factors, including depression. These factors include hopelessness, trait anger, lower self-esteem and poor self-rated problem-solving ability.(5)

In order to address this evidence, Part Two of this book focuses on symptoms of depression and cognitive factors that serve to maintain the problem. It is designed to identify a variety of feelings the young person experiences and to consider other mental health issues that contribute to their maintenance of self-harm.

References

1. Kurfoot, M., Dyer, E., Harrington, V., Woodham, A. and Harrington, R. (1996) Correlates and short term course of self-poisoning in adolescents. *British Journal of Psychiatry* 168, 38–42.
2. Meltzer, H., Harrington, R., Goodman, R. and Jenkins, R. (2001) *Children and Adolescents who Try to Harm, Hurt or Kill Themselves*. Newport: Office for National Statistics.
3. Schotte, D.E. and Clum, G.A. (1987) Problem-solving skills in suicidal psychiatric patients. *Journal of Consulting and Clinical Psychology* 55, 49–54.
4. Ellis, T.E. and Ratcliffe, K.G. (1986) Cognitive characteristics of suicidal and non-suicidal psychiatric inpatients. *Cognitive Therapy and Research* 10, 625–634.
5. Beck, A. and Steer, R.A. (1993) Dysfunctional attitudes and social ideation in psychiatric outpatients. *Suicide Life Threat Behaviour* 23, 11–20.

Session 4

This session is divided into two modules (8 and 9). Module 8 focuses on monitoring feelings and then leads to identifying thoughts and behaviours. Module 9 explores strategies to manage these.

Session 4: Cribsheet for the therapist

- Activity scheduling.
- Increasing pleasurable activities.
- Thought, feeling and behaviour links (thought triangle).

Module 8: Feelings diary review and activity scheduling

Aims

The aim of this module is to help the young person to identify their feelings, in particular sadness (depression), low self-esteem, anger and hopelessness, and to address these through behavioural activation and cognitive monitoring and restructuring. Also, the therapist should help the young person to become an expert at identifying the links between their thoughts, feelings and behaviours.

Agenda

1. Bridge from last session.
2. Homework review: feelings diary review.
3. Any issues raised by the young person (see earlier notes on this).
4. Main session topic.
5. Homework plan.
6. Feedback.

Main session topic

During the feelings diary review exercise, you will be looking at the feelings the young person has identified in their diary, discussing their intensity and frequency and any themes that recur. The idea is to take pertinent examples (situations that evoke a lot of emotion) to use in the 'help triangle' exercise.

You could use the following questions to support the discussion:

- Are the same feelings coming up a lot of the time?
- Are there certain times in the day when you feel worse? If so, what do these times have in common?
- Does it look like you are having fun in your week?
- Does it look like you get a sense of achievement in the week?

If the young person rates their mood as 'low', lists little activity in their feelings diary, or it looks like they are not getting much fun and/or achievement during the week, move on to 'Activity scheduling' before progressing to Module 9. Only if the young person perceives their mood as fine and continues to have enjoyable activities should you go straight to Module 9.

Exercise: Activity scheduling

Explain to the young person the rationale behind this exercise: the goal of activity scheduling is to maximise engagement in mood-elevating activities.(1) Explain to the young person that depression or low mood and inactivity can become a vicious circle. It slows you down, mentally and physically, and makes everything an effort. You get tired more easily, you do less, and then you blame yourself for doing less. You come to believe you can't do anything, and that you'll never get over it. That makes you even more depressed. It becomes even more difficult to do anything. And so it goes on.

Becoming more active is one way to break this vicious circle.
Being active helps you:

- to feel better and less tired;
- to motivate yourself to do more – once the day's activities are laid out in writing they will seem less overwhelming;
- to improve your ability to think;
- to structure your time and help you feel that you are taking control of your life again;
- to increase pleasurable and fun activities that are missing; and
- to make sure you have a balance between things that give you a sense of achievement as well as fun.

Look over the diary for the week with the young person, and together identify the links between times when they felt low and experienced a lack of pleasure, a lack of a sense of achievement and little activity in general. Jointly think about ideas for activities that are pleasurable to them.

Explain that you are going to put your heads together to identify *any* activities (big or small) that may be pleasurable or might have been pleasurable in the past. As well as this, you should share some of Linehan's suggestions.(2) Common examples include cooking, reading a magazine, shopping, going for a walk, drawing, phoning and going to see a friend, but a more extensive list is outlined in Table 4 and this can also be downloaded, so the young person can add their own ideas or mark up the list (Worksheet 19: Possible pleasant events). Remember to stress that the activities can be anything, however small.

Table 4 Possible pleasant events

1. Soaking in the bath	28. Cooking
2. Planning activities for the future	29. Getting a massage
3. Relaxing	30. Reminding myself of my good qualities
4. Taking some 'me' time	31. Surprising someone with a 'random act of kindness'
5. Listening to music	32. Going bowling
6. Going to watch a film	33. Doing a 'good deed for the day'
7. Going for a walk	34. Sitting in a café and people watching
8. Lying in the sun/browsing or booking a holiday	35. Going on Facebook
9. Recalling funny/happy memories	36. Doing something new
10. Laughing	37. Cuddling a pet
11. Listening to others	38. Making something
12. Reading a magazine/book	39. Painting
13. Talking to people	40. Looking at old (happy) photos
14. Going for a run	41. Changing my room around
15. Going shopping	42. Singing around the house
16. Arranging to meet a friend	43. Going out for a meal
17. Doodling	44. Doing my hair/dyeing it/straightening it
18. Looking after a plant or pet	45. Thinking that I'm an OK person
19. Meeting new people	46. Meeting up with an old friend
20. Planning what I might do if I won the lottery	47. Going ice-skating
21. Painting my nails	48. Reading jokes from a joke book
22. Writing in my diary	49. Sleeping
23. Doing a puzzle	50. Playing a musical instrument
24. Going on a picnic	51. Writing poems/stories
25. Reflecting on the day-to-day things I have achieved	52. Going to a beauty salon to have my nails done
26. Buying myself occasional treats	53. Photography
27. Talking on the phone	54. Daydreaming
	55. Watching my favourite programme

Table 4 continued

56. Going for a bike ride	67. Having an interesting discussion
57. Buying gifts	68. Positive self-talk
58. Completing a task	69. Doing some voluntary work in the community
59. Planning what a date would be like with someone I am attracted to	70. Planning where my favourite place in the world would be to visit
60. Thinking about pleasant events	71. Going somewhere different for a day
61. Doing something creative	72. Playing a game on my phone/iPad
62. Dancing	73. Going to an aquarium/museum
63. Taking the first step towards a goal	74. Looking at a nice view
64. Thinking 'I did pretty well' after doing something	75.
65. Meditating/practising mindfulness/breathing exercises	76.
	77.
66. Playing cards	78.

Source: Adapted from Linehan(3)

Explain that the young person will be completing an activity schedule about their movements during the course of the next week. This schedule is used to plan each day in advance on an hour-by-hour basis. The goal is to increase activity levels and to maximise mastery and pleasure.(4) The strategy is useful in a number of ways, but in particular it is designed to encourage an increase in the proportion of satisfying activities and promote the young person's sense of control over their life.(5) Thus, tell the young person that they will be adding at least one pleasurable activity and one activity that gives them a sense of achievement every day. Depending on the type of activity, you will decide together whether to incorporate a couple of small pleasurable/achievement activities, or one bigger one.

Next, go through Worksheet 20: Cassie's activity schedule (Table 5, which is a revised version of Table 3) and discuss it with the young person. As you will see, in italics under some of the original activities are examples of pleasurable (P) and achievement (A) activities which Cassie chose in place of her typical activities. At times, the achievement activity has been a means to manage a difficult time: for example, worry (the activity of writing down the worries to bring to the session).

After discussing Cassie's schedule, identify a few possible pleasurable activities that the young person might engage with and start to plan each day of the next week, much as Cassie did.

Download Worksheet 21: Blank activity schedule and start to complete this task together, during the session. The young person can build on this during their homework. It may not be possible to plan each day in full detail, but the young person can complete it at home, at either the beginning or the end of each day. What is important is to have a

Table 5 Cassie's activity schedule

DAY →	MONDAY
TIME ↓	
8–9 am	Lying awake in bed SAD 9 *Get up and make a cup of tea and a cooked breakfast (P)*
9–10 am	Got up late for school SAD 7
10–11 am	In English lesson WORRIED 4
11–12 pm	Still in lesson WORRIED 5 *Make a list of my worries and make every effort to turn my attention to the lesson (A)*
12–1 pm	Lunch break alone SAD 10
1–2 pm	In PE with friends WORRIED 8
2–3 pm	In English OK 5
3–4 pm	Walk home from school OK 6 *Buy magazine and sweets for later (P)*
4–5 pm	Tea with mum IRRITATED 7
5–6 pm	Up in my room MISERABLE 8 *Tidy my room and change it round (A)*
6–7 pm	Talked to my sister HAPPY 6
7–8 pm	Dinner with family BORING 7
8–9 pm	Watch TV RELAXED 8
9–10 pm	*Have a warm bubble bath with my magazine and hot chocolate (P)*
10–11 pm	Went to bed WORRY 8
11–12 am	Can't sleep WORRY 10

rough idea of both pleasure and achievement activities for each day of the forthcoming week.

Once you have done this, ask the young person whether they can think of any obstacles/problems to carrying out these activities. If they can, try to problem-solve these. It might be that the timing is wrong, or that the activity is dependent on someone else. If this is the case, work out a plan B. The following tips should help:

- Be flexible: it's just a guide. Something unexpected may happen. Keep going with it.
- Think of alternatives: have a plan A and a plan B (just in case something is not possible).
- Stick to the task in hand: just work steadily to become more active and you will eventually feel better. Don't expect it to happen all at once.
- You are always doing something, but try to think about which activities are *best* for you: sitting in a chair reading a magazine is an activity, so is lying in bed, but these may not be the activities that give you the most satisfaction.

End of Session 4

- Homework: the young person takes home the activity schedule started in the session with activities for pleasure and achievement incorporated. They will need to complete this during the week.
- Feedback.

The next module will either follow directly from the assessment of the feelings diary (for young people who are not experiencing low mood and lack of activity) or it will be introduced after the activity scheduling (for young people who are depressed).

Module 9: The help triangle

Aim

Explain that the aim of this exercise is to break down all 'emotionally loaded' situations into thoughts, feelings and behaviours on the 'help triangle'. This will allow us to identify the links and notice how each component serves to increase the negative feelings and often results in a vicious cycle of distress. At the three points of the triangle are thoughts, feelings and behaviours. The situation can be written at the top of the page, so it is clear to what the points of the triangle (the young person's reaction) are referring.

Exercise: The help triangle

Say to the young person, 'Now that we've looked at your feelings diary, it seems that you have identified feelings x, y and z quite strongly at various times during the week. Let's look at Mark's help triangle, then we'll focus on your feeling x and look at what happened around that time.'

Use Worksheet 22: Mark's help triangle (illustrated in Figure 5) to demonstrate this exercise and discuss how situations are divided into thoughts, feelings and behaviours.

Discuss Mark's situation and his interpretation of it. Ask prompt questions such as 'Could there have been a different way of seeing the situation?' and 'Do you think Mark would have felt so angry if he had thought [different interpretation]?' Point out that Mark's behaviour/ response was entirely a result of his interpretation of the event and his associated feeling of anger. He did not question his immediate automatic thoughts and got carried along with the feeling and associated behaviours, maintaining his level of anger and distress. Discuss with the young person the possible consequences of Mark's actions, including the possible thoughts and feelings he ends up with and any possible environmental consequences.

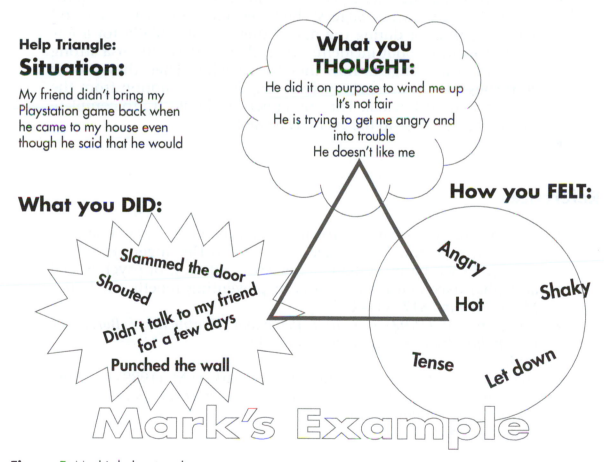

Help Triangle:

Situation:

My friend didn't bring my Playstation game back when he came to my house even though he said that he would

What you THOUGHT:

He did it on purpose to wind me up
It's not fair
He is trying to get me angry and into trouble
He doesn't like me

What you DID:

Slammed the door
Shouted
Didn't talk to my friend for a few days
Punched the wall

How you FELT:

Angry
Hot
Shaky
Tense
Let down

Mark's Example

Figure 5 Mark's help triangle

Now move on to the young person's own example. Tell them that you will be doing the same thing for one of their own real-life examples. (Note: If they haven't completed the feelings diary, discuss a fresh recent event. For example, ask, 'Can you think of a recent time when you have felt a surge of unpleasant feeling, such as anxiety, sadness, anger? More than five on the feelings scale?' Prompt to reinforce the idea that feelings, events and thoughts are different things.)

Discuss the chosen example in detail, using Worksheet 23: Blank help triangle to divide the situation into feelings, events and thoughts. The following questions should help in this process:

- What was happening when you noticed a change in your mood?
- How would you describe the emotion?
- What went through your mind?
- What was bad about this?
- What does this say about you?
- What did you do (behaviour)?

End of Session 4

- Homework: ask the young person to complete several more help triangles during the week. Suggest they keep a few copies at home and every evening (or during the day, if they can sit quietly for a few minutes) think about incidents when they noticed either a strong emotion or a change in how they were feeling. Then they should go through the process above to distinguish the emotion from the thoughts and behaviour. The young person should try to complete the triangle as close to the event as possible.
- Feedback.

References

1. Hawton, K., Arensman, E., Townsend, E., Bremner, S., Feldman, E., Goldney, R., Gunnell, D., Hazell, P. and Van Heeringen, K. (1998) Deliberate self-harm: systematic review of efficacy, of psychosocial and pharmacological treatments in preventing repetition. *British Medical Journal* 317, 441–447.
2. Linehan, M. (1993) *Cognitive Behaviour Treatment of Borderline Personality Disorder*. New York: Guilford Press.
3. Ibid.
4. Hawton, K., Salkovskis, P.M, Kirk, J. and Clark, D.M. (1989) *Cognitive Behaviour Therapy for Psychiatric Problems: A Practical Guide*. Oxford: Oxford Medical Publications.
5. Linehan, op. cit.

HANDOUT FOR THE YOUNG PERSON: SESSION 4

Activity scheduling

The goal of activity scheduling is to increase your use of mood-elevating activities. Depression or low mood and inactivity can become a vicious circle. It slows you down, mentally and physically, and makes everything an effort. You get tired more easily, you do less and you blame yourself for doing less. You come to believe you *can't* do anything and that you'll *never* get over it. That makes you even more depressed. It becomes even more difficult to do anything. And so it goes on.

Becoming more active is one way to break the circle.

Activity helps you:

- to feel better and less tired;
- to motivate yourself to do more – once the day's activities are laid out in writing they will seem less overwhelming;
- to improve your ability to think;
- to structure your time and help you feel that you are taking control of your life again;
- to increase pleasurable and fun activities that are missing; and
- to make sure you have a balance between things that give you a sense of achievement as well as fun.

Remember:

- Be flexible: it's just a guide. Something unexpected may happen. Keep going with it.
- Think of alternatives: have a plan A and a plan B (just in case something is not possible).
- Stick to the task in hand: just work steadily to become more active and you will eventually feel better. Don't expect it to happen all at once.
- You are always doing something, but try to think about which activities are *best* for you: sitting in a chair reading a magazine is an activity, so is lying in bed, but these may not be the activities that give you the most satisfaction.

Session 5

Session 5: Cribsheet for the therapist

- Negative automatic thoughts (NATs).
- Identifying and recognising cognitive bias.

Module 10: Negative automatic thoughts (NATs)

Aim

The aim of this module is to become a 'thought detective', especially to understand what NATs are and to recognise when they arise, their links with emotions and particular themes of NATs that the young person experiences. Note: if you did not have time to introduce the help triangle (Module 9) in Session 4, start with that now.

Agenda

- Bridge from last session.
- Homework review.
- Any issues raised by the young person.
- Main session topic.
- Homework plan.
- Feedback.

Main session topic

Remind the young person of the central principle of Cognitive Behaviour Therapy: that the ways in which an individual behaves are determined by immediate situations, and the individual's interpretations of those situations.(1) Explain to the young person that our minds are always busy. It can seem like there is a 'running commentary' in our heads as we do things if we pay attention to our thoughts. We think about all sorts of things, what is happening around us, about ourselves and other people. These thoughts can be positive or negative (or both), but when we are feeling low or under-confident, they can be extremely negative and persistent. We all think like this from time to time but when we are feeling especially low, depressed, or anxious, the tendency is for our thinking to become extremely negatively biased. At these times, our thoughts are negative, habitual and quick, and, therefore, they can be difficult to identify. The fact that they are automatic and involuntary means they can also be hard to 'control'.(2)

A particular problem that tends to exacerbate low mood is that thoughts can be unhelpful and plausible, especially when accompanying emotions are strong, and so may be difficult to challenge. We call these NATs (negative automatic thoughts). These can be triggered by many things (including therapy itself) and must be identified and addressed as they have a direct impact on our emotions and behaviours and tend to make us feel even more distressed. The thoughts are often taken as facts, so they are believed and tend to make distressing emotions last longer.

Explain to the young person that NATs are due to biases in the way we process information. This means that we are seeing the world through a type of 'negative filter'; in other words, our perceptions and interpretations of experience are distorted. Sometimes the perception makes sense but it may be too far in one direction.

These thoughts may be about the way we see ourselves:

- I'm fat.
- I have lots of friends.
- I am very moody.
- (People think) I'm funny.

They may be about how we judge and 'comment' on what we do:

- I'm no good at revision.
- I'm quite sociable.
- I'm good at listening to other people's problems.

They may describe our view of the future:

- No one will ever want to go out with me.
- I'll fail my exams.
- I will be a professional footballer.

A key part of trying to manage our feelings is to become a sort of 'thought detective' and to start to recognise the thoughts that appear when we feel strong emotions. In order to feel better, we need to recognise our thoughts and then try to disentangle helpful and unhelpful thoughts and question the validity of some of the repetitive negative thoughts.

At this stage, you can go back to Worksheet 5: What is CBT? and use that to discuss the link between thoughts and feelings, as appropriate.

Show the young person Cassie's NATs about herself, the future and others and discuss them, then complete the exercise below to help them identify some of their own NATs.

SOME OF CASSIE'S NEGATIVE THOUGHTS ABOUT HERSELF, THE FUTURE AND OTHERS

I am no good at school-work.

I'm going to fail my exams.

No one cares about or loves me.

Exercise: Identify your NATs

For this exercise, read through the outlined problem scenario and think together about what the emotional, physical and behavioural reactions the young person might have. Following this, think about what automatic thoughts the young person has that link with the reactions they have given.

Problem

You are sitting at school eating lunch with a friend when one of your teachers walks by and says to you in an irritated tone, 'Please come and see me in my office as soon as you have finished your lunch.'

What reactions might you have?

- Emotional
- Physical
- Behavioural

What automatic thoughts might you have?

When you feel that the young person can identify NATs, either work through another blank help triangle, or use a recent event (or help triangle example), and ask them to identify the NATs from their thoughts. Again, highlight the thoughts, emotions and behaviours in the appropriate sections.

The next step is to consolidate this skill and continue completing real-life examples. Depending on time, you can either continue with examples during the session or set this as a homework task.

Continue to practise using the help triangle. Take everyday examples of feeling surges or switches and fill in more triangles during the week.

End of Session 5

- Homework: help triangles.
- Feedback.

References

1. Hawton, K., Salkovskis, P.M., Kirk, J. and Clark D.M. (1989) *Cognitive Behaviour Therapy for Psychiatric Problems: A Practical Guide*. Oxford: Oxford Medical Publications.
2. Ibid.

HANDOUT FOR THE YOUNG PERSON: SESSION 5

Negative automatic thoughts (NATs)

Remember that the main principle of Cognitive Behaviour Therapy is that the ways in which an individual behaves are determined by immediate situations, and the individual's interpretations of those situations. Our minds are always busy. It can seem like there is a 'running commentary' in our heads as we do things if we pay attention to our thoughts. We think about all sorts of things, what is happening around us, about ourselves and other people. These thoughts can be positive or negative (or both), but when we are feeling low or under-confident, they can be extremely negative and persistent. We all think like this from time to time but when we are feeling especially low, depressed or anxious, the tendency is for our thinking to become extremely negatively biased. At these times, our thoughts are negative, habitual and quick, so can be difficult to identify. The fact that they are automatic and involuntary means they can also be hard to 'control'.

A particular problem that tends to make low moods worse is that the thoughts can be unhelpful and believable, especially when accompanying emotions are strong, so they may be difficult to challenge. We call these thoughts NATs (negative automatic thoughts). These can be triggered by many things (including therapy itself) and must be identified and addressed as they have a direct impact on our emotions and behaviours and tend to make us feel even more distressed. The thoughts are often taken as facts, so they are believed and tend to make distressing emotions last longer.

NATs are due to a bias in the way we process information. This means that we are seeing the world through a type of 'negative filter'; in other words, our perceptions and interpretations of experience are distorted.

These thoughts may be about the way we see ourselves:

- I'm fat.
- I have lots of friends.
- I am very moody.
- (People think) I'm funny.

They may be about how we judge and 'comment' on what we do:

- I'm no good at revision.
- I'm quite sociable.
- I'm good at listening to other people's problems.

They may describe our view of the future:

- No one will ever want to go out with me.
- I'll fail my exams.
- I will be a professional footballer.

A key part of trying to manage our feelings is to become a sort of 'thought detective' and to start to recognise the thoughts that appear when we feel strong emotions. In order to feel better, we need to recognise our thoughts and then try to disentangle helpful and unhelpful thoughts and question the truth behind some of the repetitive negative thoughts.

Session 6

This session comprises one module, Module 11, which focuses on thought distortions and thought-challenging.

Session 6: Cribsheet for the therapist

- Thought distortions.
- Thought-challenging.
- Completing a thought record.

Module 11: Thought distortions and thought-challenging

Aim

To identify thinking distortions/pitfalls and introduce thought-challenging, including evidence for and against a thought and alternative, more adaptive ways of thinking.

Agenda

- Bridge from last session.
- Homework review: help triangles. Ask the young person, 'How did it go?' Were there any problems? Look for mixing up thoughts and emotions and what they've noticed from the practice.
- Any issues raised by the young person.
- Main session topic.
- Homework plan.
- Feedback.

Main session topic: Thought distortions

Explain to the young person that now that they have some experience in identifying their thoughts, highlighting their NATs and recognising the impact negative thoughts can have on emotions and behaviours, we are going to look at ways to break this cycle and challenge the NATs.

Note: some people may feel more depressed than usual at this stage as they are being asked to focus on the negative. Explain that this may happen and that it will be quickly addressed as they learn techniques to manage these thoughts.

Look again at their homework (examples of help triangles) or complete a few more help triangles in the session, drawn from situations the young person has experienced in the preceding week/weeks. Continue to identify and pick out themes of thoughts that keep arising by asking, 'Can you see any thoughts/types of thinking that come up again and again?'

Tell the young person that we sometimes muddle up thoughts with facts and might accept them without question. Explain that the expression 'looking through rose-tinted spectacles' is used to describe someone who always sees things in a hopeful or cheerful way, even when they are bad. This is a kind of thought distortion or thinking bias because it is unrealistic. The person sees the situation from only one viewpoint and does not see the negative aspects of it. Conversely, someone else might see things only from a negative perspective: 'My friend never rang. Nobody ever wants to talk or listen to me.'

Thought distortions or thinking biases are common and unhelpful ways of thinking. Everyone makes these distortions, but when they happen regularly, they can make you feel bad and affect your decisions about things and how you behave. A useful strategy is to learn to analyse these thoughts and challenge them, both to test out if they are true or not and to help you feel better. There are many different types of thinking bias, which you should now discuss further. The five distortions listed below are the main ones to look out for, although there are many others, too.

Exercise: Thought distortions

Download Worksheet 24: Glasses and Worksheet 25: Thinking pitfalls to illustrate and prompt discussion of the five main distortions. Go through each example in turn, highlighting the glasses analogy. For example, in 'black-and-white' thinking, the person has the black-and-white glasses and interprets situations in an 'all-or-nothing' way (see Katy's example).

BLACK-AND-WHITE THINKING: KATY

Katy had an argument with a good friend and thought, 'That's it, I'm not friends with her any more. I'm never going to speak to her again.'

As you look at the various thinking pitfalls, get the young person to think about a time when they might have fallen into each particular thinking trap. Use their help triangles homework to find their personal thinking pitfalls.

1. Black-and-white thinking. Looking at things in an 'all-or-nothing' way: for example, someone who sees things as either wonderful or terrible, total success or complete failure, with nothing in between.
2. Jumping to conclusions. When you conclude that things are going to go wrong, or you have done something wrong, without considering possible alternative explanations. Thinking that you know how someone else thinks or feels ('mind-reading') or thinking that you know what will happen ('fortune-telling'): for example, not sitting a test because you 'know' you will fail or thinking that someone no longer likes you because they did not say hello.
3. Over-generalising. Blowing things out of proportion. You can often spot these when there is an 'always', 'never', 'everyone' or 'no one' in the thought: for example, getting a bad grade and thinking, 'Everyone else is better than me. I am never any good at anything.'
4. Should/must/ought. Giving yourself a hard time: 'I must do better', 'I should be better', 'I ought to have known better'. These are often linked with over-generalisations: 'I should always', etc.
5. Blaming yourself. When you feel responsible for things that are not your fault or that are beyond your control: for example, 'My dad left because of my behaviour', 'It is my fault that I got beaten up', etc.

Tell the young person not to worry if all of the above sound familiar. Explain that these are all thinking biases that everyone makes. You may find that you do one more than the others or that you combine several types of thinking bias.

Main session topic: Thought-challenging

Thinking biases can make us experience some unpleasant feelings, such as sadness, anger, etc. Sometimes we are so self-critical that we start to accept these thoughts as true facts. Checking these thoughts out, and challenging them to test whether they are true, can help to stop them going round and round in our heads. If we don't challenge them, we can end up feeling worse.

Remind the young person again that what we think affects how we feel and what we do. Explain that challenging our thoughts is more than just thinking positively about life; it is about having *balanced thinking*, which involves looking for evidence to *support and challenge* our thoughts.

Exercise: Thought-challenging

Consult the feelings diary the young person completed and/or one of the help triangles they did for homework or find a new example. Highlight one negative automatic thought, the more extreme the better: for example, 'I'm useless at everything.' Be careful to choose a thought that is about the young person, as these thoughts tend to be more powerful and prone to distortions based on young people's beliefs about themselves, others and the world. It is not a good idea to try to challenge a thought about another person at this stage (as we don't know the whole story), so avoid thoughts such as: 'Sarah doesn't like me.'

When you have identified a thought, explain to the young person that you will be looking for evidence for and against it. Make two columns on a piece of paper, with one side evidence for and the other side evidence against. Ask the young person to identify all the evidence for the thought being true by explaining the reasons why they believe that thought to be true. Really try to stretch the young person to tell you *every* reason – including such nebulous concepts as having a 'feeling' – as well as their previous experiences linked with the thought. The aim is to get everything down now to avoid later 'yes . . . buts'. It is important that this stage is done thoroughly so that the young person has a chance to say why this thought keeps recurring. Although they may feel like they are re-experiencing the unwelcome emotion, it can be very validating to hear it in this way.

In the second column (evidence against), instruct the young person to look for and record any evidence that challenges their thought. Tell them that they are now thinking of evidence that goes against the specific thought: for example, the idea that they are 'useless at everything'. This is often the hardest part of the exercise and may require more prompting. Ask what alternative explanations there might be, ask them to think what someone else (who knows the young person) might suggest as evidence against this thought.

After they have identified all the evidence against, spend some time reading both columns back to the young person. Ask them what they make of the exercise and what they are thinking now. Can they re-rate their belief in this thought now? Then ask if they can identify a more balanced thought or alternative – less negative – interpretation of the same thought based on this exercise. This is also an opportunity (if they have not done so earlier) to identify which type of thinking bias(es) this thought might be.

Exercise: The thought record

Download Worksheet 26: The thought record and explain that this is a more advanced version of the help triangle. It is divided into ten columns, with key symbols for most columns. The advancement from the help triangle is in the strategy of challenging the NAT, as you have just done in the previous exercise. After looking at the instructions and Katy's example, start to fill in the columns one by one, using the earlier example.

Explain to the young person that the thought record should be used when they next experience an unpleasant mood or troubling thought. As you fill it in, discuss each column in turn.

- *Situation*. Where were you? What were you doing? When? With whom?
- *Feelings*. Use one word to describe each of your feelings at the time. Rate how strong each was using the feelings scale (0–10).
- *Thoughts*. Describe any thoughts you noticed going through your mind. Highlight at least one NAT from the example and write it in the column.

It might be useful to try to elicit further thoughts at this stage by exploring the meaning of the thought with the young person. You could ask questions such as: 'If that were true, what does that mean to you/say about you?'

- *Beliefs*. Next, ask the young person to rate how much they believe that thought as a percentage (100 per cent = believe it to be true without any doubt; 0 per cent = believe it is totally untrue). The young person may describe believing it 100 per cent at the time but now being less sure (for example, 80 per cent). This is useful information to support the tendency for high negative emotion at the time to cause us to rationalise less and believe negative thoughts more. Write down both levels of belief prior to looking at evidence for and against the thought. You can use the belief scale to record the level of belief and download Worksheet 27: The belief scale).
- *Balancing*. The next step is for the young person to record evidence that they can see supports their thoughts. After they have identified all the evidence against, ask them to work on the steps 6–9.
- *Thinking distortions/bias*. Looking back at their NATs, can the young person spot any thinking biases/exaggerations in their thinking?
- *Beliefs again*. Now the young person should re-rate the percentage of their belief in each thought. Have these changed?
- *Alternative thoughts*. Now that the young person is able to perceive their thought in a more balanced way, they should try to come up with an alternative – more carefully considered or balanced – thought.
- *Feelings again*. Finally, the young person should think about whether their feelings have changed and record this.

It can sometimes be helpful to imagine someone (such as a best friend, sister or brother) and think, 'If they had this problem/thought, what would I say to them about what they were thinking?'

Download Worksheet 28: Quick reference guide to help with completion of the thought record, and see Katy's thought record for an example (Table 6, and download Worksheet 29: Sample thought record – Katy's situation).

Download Worksheet 30: Help with challenging yourself.

Table 6 Sample thought record – Katy's situation

Situation	What were you feeling? Scale rating	What thoughts were going through your mind? (NATs)	How much do you believe thoughts? %	What evidence supports your belief in these thoughts?	What evidence challenges your belief?	Can you spot thinking pitfalls?	How much do you believe thoughts now? %	Possible alternative thoughts	How do you rate feelings now?
Argument with my best friend	Angry (100%) Hurt (90%) Cheated (75%)	I'm unvalued. I have never meant any-thing to her. I'm pathetic.	100% 80% 60%	She often makes me feel worthless. She seems to pick fights to upset me and break our friendship.	We are both strong personalities with different ideas. Afterwards, we can laugh about the disagreement.	Over-generalising	60%	It's OK to disagree. I can still be important to someone even (especially?) if we argue.	Angry (40%) Hurt (60%) Cheated (30%)

End of Session 6

- Homework: the young person should complete the thought record during the forthcoming week with a real-life example, and have a go at challenging the thought. They can use Worksheet 28: Quick reference guide to help. Explain that thought identification and especially thought-challenging take time and practice, so this is just a start. You do not expect them to be an expert immediately: it takes at least two weeks for adults to start to understand the concept. They can leave some columns blank if the task is becoming too difficult, and you will go through the thought record with them during the next session and try to fill in the gaps. The important thing is to try to identify an example during the week when they have noticed a surge of emotion, to write down the situation, to break their response into emotions, thoughts and behaviours, and to have a go at finding evidence for and against a key NAT.
- Feedback.

HANDOUT FOR THE YOUNG PERSON: SESSION 6

How to break the cycle of thoughts and negative feelings

Sometimes we muddle up thoughts with facts and we might accept them without question. The expression 'looking through rose-tinted spectacles' is used to describe someone who always sees things in a hopeful or cheerful way, even when they are bad. This is a kind of thought distortion or bias because it is unrealistic or extreme. The person sees the situation from only one viewpoint; they do not see the negative aspects.

Thought distortions or thought biases are common and unhelpful ways of thinking. Everyone makes these distortions, but when they happen regularly they can make you feel bad and affect your decisions about things and how you behave. A useful strategy is to learn to analyse these thoughts and challenge them, both to test out if they are true and to help you feel better.

There are many different types of thinking bias, but the five main ones are listed below:

- Black-and-white thinking. Looking at things in an 'all-or-nothing' way: for example, someone who sees things as either wonderful or terrible, total success or complete failure, with nothing in between.
- Jumping to conclusions. Thinking that you know how someone else thinks or feels ('mind-reading') or thinking that you know what will happen ('fortune-telling'): for example, not sitting a test because you 'know' you will fail or thinking that someone no longer likes you because they did not say hello.
- Over-generalising. Blowing things out of proportion. You can often spot these when there is an 'always', 'never', 'everyone' or 'no one' in the thought: for example, getting a bad grade and thinking, 'Everyone else is better than me. I am never any good at anything.'
- Should/must/ought. Giving yourself a hard time: 'I must do better', 'I should be better', 'I ought to have known better'. These thoughts are often linked with over-generalisations: 'I should always . . .', etc.
- Blaming yourself. When you feel responsible for things that are not your fault or that are beyond your control: 'My dad left because of my behaviour', 'It is my fault that I got beaten up', etc.

Thought-challenging

Thinking biases can make us experience some unpleasant feelings, such as sadness, anger, etc. Sometimes we are so self-critical that we start to accept these thoughts as true facts. Checking out such thoughts, and challenging them to test whether they are true, can help to stop them going round and round in our heads. If we don't challenge them, we can end up feeling worse.

Challenging your thoughts is not just about thinking positively about life; it is about having *balanced thinking*, which involves looking for evidence to support and challenge your thoughts.

Completing the thought record

- *Situation.* Where were you? What were you doing? When? With whom?
- *Feelings.* Use one word to describe each of your feelings at the time. Rate how strong each one is using the feelings scale (0–10).
- *Thoughts.* Describe any thoughts you noticed going through your mind. Highlight at least one negative automatic thought (NAT) from the example and write it in the column. If it were true, what does it mean to you/say about you?
- *Beliefs.* Rate how much you believe that thought as a percentage (with 100 per cent = believe it to be true without a doubt and 0 per cent = believe it is totally untrue).
- *Balancing.* The next step is to write down all the evidence that supports your thought. Then, look for and record any evidence that goes against the thought.
- *Thinking distortions.* Look back at your NATs. Can you spot any thinking biases/ exaggerations in the thinking, etc.?
- *Beliefs again.* Now re-rate the percentage of your belief in each thought. Has it changed?
- *Alternative thoughts.* Now that you are seeing your thought in a more balanced way, try to come up with an alternative – more carefully considered or balanced – thought.
- *Feelings again.* Think about whether your feelings have changed and record this.

It can sometimes help to imagine someone (a best friend, sister or brother) and think, 'If they had the same problem/thought, what would I say to them about how they were thinking?'

Session 7

This session continues to focus on Module 11. However, if you find that this does not fill the session, then Module 12 can be incorporated. Module 12 is the formulation, and it is linked with the eliciting of core beliefs and rules for living covered in Module 11.

Session 7: Cribsheet for the therapist

- Formulation.
- Core beliefs and rules for living.

Module 12: Beyond the help triangle: core beliefs and rules for living

Aim

If the young person is more insightful, very depressed or older, with well-established patterns of behaviour and recurring NATs, it can be useful to identify their core beliefs.

Agenda

- Bridge from last session.
- Homework review: thought record. Review this and spend time working on it if the young person has encountered problems. Encourage them to keep going with this over the next few weeks.
- Any issues raised by the young person.
- Main session topic.
- Homework plan.
- Feedback.

Main session topic

Explain to the young person that there are three different levels of interpretation when anyone encounters a situation. First, there are the automatic thoughts (discussed in the last session), which usually appear as verbal statements (or images) in our heads. The second level includes 'rules for living' or conditional assumptions. These are much less obvious than automatic thoughts and we can figure them out only by looking closely at our actions. Look at Katy's example.

CONDITIONAL ASSUMPTIONS: KATY

'A girl in the year above me disagreed with my opinion during the discussion we had after school. I immediately felt bad and thought, "They don't like me and they think I'm stupid."'
In this case, Katy's assumption might be either:

- *if* people disagree with me, *then* they don't like me

or

- other people's opinions are more important than mine.

You can see how these assumptions consist of more than mere statements; they involve beliefs about how certain situations have meaning to the person. Assumptions often occur as 'if . . . then' statements and sound like general rules. This will make more sense later, after core beliefs are explained.

Ask the young person to hold on to this as a concept but reassure them that you will be explaining in more detail after focusing on core beliefs – the third and deepest level of cognition.

Core beliefs

Core beliefs are seemingly unquestionable opinions about ourselves, others or the world. Explain to the young person that when we are growing up, we develop these beliefs on the basis of both our actual experiences and our perception of our experiences. Greenberger and Padesky refer to the theory that young babies start to make sense of their world by organising their experiences into familiar patterns.(1) These patterns that develop, which are seen as rules and beliefs about the world around them, are not necessarily reflections of the 'true' environment but instead the consequence of an underdeveloped mental ability in the young child that is rather rigid and inflexible. As we grow up, most of the 'rules' we have developed during our childhood become more fluid and flexible as we see exceptions and alternative explanations. However, some of our childhood beliefs stay absolute even into adulthood.

When we think the same thoughts about ourselves over and over again, and repetitively judge what we do, those thoughts and beliefs grow stronger and more fixed. As well as this, when early life experiences recur or are extremely traumatic, we can become convinced that this will continue to happen. This perception can start to rule our lives because the thoughts are often extremely negative and become too strong and plausible to challenge.

The second reinforcer of such beliefs is the information-processing bias that follows. In other words, any new evidence that contradicts the beliefs tends to be ignored or dismissed as unimportant and untrue, as it does not fit with our perception of reality; essentially, it is filtered out.

Core beliefs tend not to be in our heads all the time (or ever). Rather, they seem to be held below consciousness and manifest only occasionally as short, brief statements: for example, 'I am lovable' or 'I am worthless'. If beliefs are negative – for example, 'I'm a failure' – they often make you feel bad and can filter the way you see the world. If a person thinks that negative things are going to happen because of a flaw in them, then this can set them up to fail. A good example is if someone believes that no one will ever love them (they feel unlovable), they may reject any signs of affection from parents, friends or boy/girlfriends and feel that none of these people really cares, or that they have an ulterior motive for expressing affection. This might stop people from showing affection, and the belief that the person is unlovable will be strengthened.

Part of the information-processing bias is that anything that supports the negative core belief, however trivial, is seized upon as 'proof' of its veracity. As well as this, because core beliefs help us to make sense of our world at a young age, it may never occur to us to evaluate whether there are more useful ways to understand our current experiences. Instead, as adolescents (and into adulthood), a person might act, think and feel as if these beliefs are 100 per cent true.

CASSIE'S CORE BELIEFS

- Everything I do must be perfect.
- I always get things wrong – I'm a failure.
- I'm unlovable.

Exercise: Core beliefs

Look at Cassie's core beliefs and ask the young person which dangers/difficulties she might experience by holding on to them. (For example, by believing that everything she does must be perfect, she might avoid trying new things because of a fear of failure; or she might judge herself harshly whenever she doesn't obtain a top grade at school.)

Exercise: Rules of living

It is now time to return to the 'rules of living' that were introduced earlier. Remind the young person that core beliefs are so entrenched that they can influence the decisions we make. This means that they can lead us to develop certain rules and patterns of living. Go through two examples: 'I'm not good enough' and 'I'm unlovable and no one will ever love me'.

'I'm not good enough'

The belief that 'I'm not good enough', which may arise from living in a home where achievement is valued over and above anything else (or is perceived to be), may lead a person to develop the rule that they will be successful only if they do everything really well or even perfectly. This might result in stress and unhappiness as each piece of work is repeated over and over again or perhaps never even started.

This is an example of how a core belief – 'I'm not good enough' – can trigger an automatic thought and an assumption – for example, 'I'm stupid' – and create a rule of living: 'there's no point in even starting my schoolwork'.

THE RULES OF LIVING BROUGHT ABOUT BY CASSIE'S CORE BELIEFS

- There's no point in even starting my assignment as it won't be good enough (done perfectly).
- People will like me only if I do what they want me to do.
- If I'm successful, then I'll be happy.

Ask the young person to identify the dangers for Cassie of following these rules.

'I'm unlovable and no one will ever love me'

The belief that 'I'm unlovable and no one will ever love me' might lead a person to assume that others don't really want to spend time with them, so they will probably feel sad and avoid other people. Avoiding other people means that they have no chance to experience others showing that they like them and want to be around them. This in turn could lead to others thinking that the person doesn't want to be friends with them, so they might start to avoid them too. This strengthens the person's conviction that their belief is true.

In this example, the core belief 'I'm unlovable' has led to the assumption 'people don't want to be around me' and caused the rule of living 'avoid other people, as they don't want to be around me'. In turn, this has strengthened the core belief.

Discuss this vicious circle with the young person.

Exercise: The pen-friend, or new Facebook friend

Download Worksheet 31: The pen-friend, or new Facebook friend and explain to the young person that you are going to try to identify their core beliefs and rules of living. Ask them to imagine that they are writing to a pen-friend, someone they have never met, so they need to provide a description of themselves. Explain that the idea is to think 'off the cuff': there are no right or wrong answers and the description should be based on 'gut feeling'.

On the worksheet, use the following prompts and then fill in the details (which can be discussed together):

- I am . . .
- Other people see me as . . .
- Other people are . . .
- Relationships are . . .
- The world is . . .
- The future is . . .

Pull together the previously completed thought records and help triangles and ask the young person to think about the themes that come up for them. What do they think their core beliefs might be and what are their associated rules for living?

End of Session 7

- Homework: continue with thought records and the identification of core beliefs and associated rules of living.
- Feedback.

Reference

1. Greenberger, D. and Padesky, C.A. (1995) *Mind over Mood: Change How You Feel by Changing the Way You Think*. New York: Guilford Press.

HANDOUT FOR THE YOUNG PERSON: SESSION 7

There are three levels of understanding when you encounter a situation.

Automatic thoughts

These usually appear as words (or images) in our heads.

'Rules for living' or conditional assumptions

These are much less obvious than automatic thoughts. We can figure them out only by looking closely at our actions. Look at Katy's example.

KATY'S RULES FOR LIVING

'A girl in the year above me disagreed with my opinion during the discussion we had after school. I immediately felt sh** and thought, "They don't like me and they think I'm stupid."'

In this case, Katy's assumption might be either:

• If people disagree with me, then they don't like me

or

• other people's opinions are more important than mine.

Assumptions often occur as 'if . . . then' statements and sound like general rules.

Core beliefs

These develop from our beliefs about the world, others and ourselves that we pick up as we grow up. They are based on both our actual experiences and our perception of our experiences. CBT is based on the theory that young babies start to make sense of their world by organising their experiences into familiar patterns. These patterns that develop, which are seen as rules and beliefs about the world, are not necessarily reflections of the 'true' environment; instead, they come from the child's perception of what is going on. Young children tend to think in quite rigid ways, which become more flexible as they grow up. This is why core beliefs are quite strong statements that sound like facts.

When we think the same thoughts about ourselves over and over again, and keep judging what we do, the thoughts and beliefs become stronger and more fixed. Also, when early life experiences recur or are extremely traumatic, they can start to influence how we view life and can begin to rule our lives. Such thoughts are often extremely negative and become too strong and plausible to challenge.

These core beliefs are also strengthened because any new evidence that goes against them tends to be ignored or dismissed as unimportant and untrue, because it does not fit with our reality; essentially, it is filtered out.

Core beliefs tend not to be in our heads all the time (or ever). Instead, they seem to be held below consciousness and appear only occasionally as short, brief statements: for example, 'I am lovable' or 'I am worthless'. If beliefs are negative – for example, 'I'm a failure' – they often make you feel bad and can filter the way you see the world. If you think that negative things are going to happen because of a flaw in yourself, then this can set you up to fail. A good example is if someone believes that no one will ever love them (they feel unlovable), they might reject any signs of affection from parents, friends or boy/girlfriends and think that these people don't really care, or that they have an ulterior motive for expressing affection. In turn, this might stop those people from showing affection, which will strengthen the person's belief that they are unlovable.

Examples

'I'm not good enough'

The belief that 'I'm not good enough', which may arise from living in a home where achievement is valued over and above anything else, may lead a person to develop the rule that they will be successful only if they do everything really well or even perfectly. This might result in stress and unhappiness as each piece of work is repeated over and over again or perhaps never even started.

This is an example of how a core belief – 'I'm not good enough' – can trigger an automatic thought and assumption – for example, 'I'm stupid' – and create a rule of living: 'there's no point in even starting my schoolwork'.

'I'm unlovable and no one will ever love me'

The belief that 'I'm unlovable and no one will ever love me' might lead you to assume that people don't really want to spend time with you, so you will probably feel sad and avoid other people. Avoiding other people means that they have no chance to show they like you and want to be around you, and they may actually start to think that you don't want to be friends with them, so they will start to avoid you, too. This strengthens your conviction that your belief is true.

In this example, the core belief 'I'm unlovable' has led to the assumption 'people don't want to be around me' and caused the rule of living 'avoid other people, as they don't want to be around me'. In turn, this has strengthened the core belief . . . and so the vicious cycle continues.

Session 8

As mentioned at the start of the previous session, Module 12 can be delivered in Session 7, if you have time. If not, it should be delivered now, along with Module 13, an extension of 12.

Session 8: Cribsheet for the therapist

- Formulation.

Module 13: Formulation – 'my journey'

Aim

To piece together why problems have started, what maintains them and where they might have originated. This is the cognitive behavioural formulation.

Agenda

- Bridge from last session.
- Homework review.
- Any issues raised by the young person.
- Main session topic.
- Review of problems and measures (see end of session notes).
- Homework plan.
- Feedback.

Main session topic

Earlier modules have focused on the individual components of the formulation, such as core beliefs, NATs and rules for living. Explain to the young person that it is useful to think about how all of these fit together, something we call 'formulation'. In this collaborative process, the aim is to piece together how the young person has become who they are, and understand why they experience the world in the way that they do. It's a bit like making a map of their life. Explain that it can sometimes feel uncomfortable to revisit the past because it can dredge up unpleasant memories, but it can also be a very helpful process to help us understand what makes them unique, to identify their 'danger spots', and to stop them from falling into them again and again.

Further explanation of the process of Cognitive Behaviour Therapy is useful here. Start by saying that there is increasing evidence that what we experience in our early lives (maybe even from the time when we are babies) is programmed into our minds and leads us to have certain beliefs about ourselves, the world, other people and the future. These implanted beliefs help us to process information efficiently and allow us to make sense of a rapidly changing world. When we are very young, this is quite a good thing, as, for example, it would be very tiring (and a very inefficient use of our brains) if every time we looked at a chair we had to relearn what it was and what it was used for.

However, if, for example, a young child feels scared when they are near certain people, they might start to believe that 'other people are dangerous', and this belief might then start to dictate their behaviour. Alternatively, if they start to believe that they are being compared unfavourably with a sibling who has different skills, they might start to believe that 'other people are more successful than me' or 'I'm no good'.

Thus, core beliefs are established when we are very young and continue to be established and strengthened as we grow up, and these can lead to certain rules of living that we follow, sometimes without even knowing that we are doing it. Sometimes, a specific event might 'activate' a core belief: for example, a person who feels 'unlovable' might become depressed when a relationship breaks down. This, in turn, will lead to an upsurge of NATs and behaviours that reinforce the core belief.

To illustrate this process, look at Jessica's formulation (Worksheet 32: Jessica's formulation).

JESSICA'S FORMULATION

Why me?

- Early experiences: Grandmother died; parents divorced and difficult relationships with Dad; sister was the 'golden child'; I was bullied at school; Mum was depressed; at home there was lack of expression of emotion and no arguments.
- My beliefs and rules of living (based on pen-friend exercise and early experiences): I'm not good enough; I'm unlovable; other people's needs always come first; if people disagree with me, then they don't like me, or their opinions are more important than mine.

continued

Why now?

What happened before (my problems got really bad)?

- Broke up with my girlfriend.

Why still?

What keeps my problems going?

- Avoid going out.
- Don't get close to anyone.
- Don't tell people how I'm feeling.

Good stuff

What helps?

- Listening to music.
- Cousin phoning.
- Forcing myself to go to friend's (small) party.
- My positive self-statements and challenges to my crucial thoughts.

Exercise: My journey

Download Worksheet 33: My Journey and start to fill in the young person's own formulation. Explain that there are no wrong or right answers and sometimes they will have to guess. This is just the start of the process and it will evolve over time, as we look at the young person's 'journey' in more detail over the next few sessions. The journey proceeds from the young person's early experiences, to their core beliefs and rules of living, to 'Why now?' and 'Why still?', before concluding with the 'Good stuff' that helps them to manage their current life.

Tell the young person that they should begin with their early experiences. This is the moment when everything they have told you previously about their childhood should be written down. They should include significant life events, parental break-ups, mental health problems in the family, bullying, etc. Useful prompt questions include:

- Can you think of any happy and sad memories from your childhood?
- What was the atmosphere like at home when you were younger?
- What is your mum/dad/sibling/carer like? Can you describe them?
- What were you like as a younger child?
- How was school? What were your parents' views on academic success, homework, etc.?
- What were the rules like at home? Was there much discipline?
- Did people show their emotions or hide them?

Explain that there might be some gaps, but as new memories arise and new insights occur additions or changes can be made to the boxes at any time, as appropriate.

It can be useful to start by writing in key issues that the young person feels are highly relevant to their story. Ask if they feel that certain events/issues in their life are particularly relevant. They might reflect on their childhood and remember specific incidents, but might not know if these are relevant to their formulation at this stage. This is a learning phase for both the therapist and the young person, so it is fine to write some ideas in pencil or outside the boxes if you cannot find obvious places for them within the formulation.

Next you should move on to the beliefs section. Ask the young person: 'What kind of beliefs might someone who has experienced the things in your early experiences box have about the world, others and himself/herself?' One way of accessing the young person's core beliefs and rules for living is to look through their thought record. Looking at recurring themes that arise might help you to come up with core beliefs and rules of living collaboratively. Another way is to use the 'downward arrow' technique. For this, you take one of the young person's negative thoughts and ask them, 'What does this situation mean or say about you?' and 'If this were true, what would be so bad about that?'.(1) The question 'What does this mean or say about you?' should then be repeated after each of the young person's answers (a bit like peeling away the layers of an onion), until you arrive at their core belief. For two examples of this process, see Figures 6 and 7 (Worksheets 34: Mark's core belief and 35: Cassie's core belief).

Figure 6 Mark's core belief

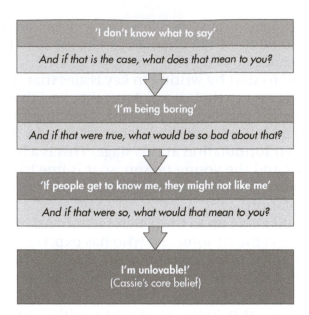

Figure 7 Cassie's core belief

The rules of living are identified by picking up patterns of behaviours and linking them with the core belief. Ask the young person:

- What things they do to protect themselves from their core belief coming true.
- To complete an 'if . . . then . . .' sentence. (In Cassie's example, you might have asked, 'If you get close to someone, then . . .?' and Cassie would need to think about what comes next.)

Move on to the 'Why now?' section and ask the young person what happened before the problems started to get really bad. Was there a particular trigger? Why did things slip into the way they are now?

Once you have completed 'Why now?' go on to 'Why still?' This section looks at maintaining factors. It can be completed once the young person starts to gain an insight into why their self-harm has developed into a cycle. The idea is to understand the behaviours and responses from others that maintain the problems.

The exercise concludes with the 'Good stuff'. In this section, the aim is to identify all of the positive things with which the young person is engaging. Include protective factors, such as friendships, going out, hobbies, interests and the functional management of emotions or tricky situations.

Remember that this is just the start of formulation. It is an ongoing process that you will be conducting with the young person throughout the remaining modules and you will refer to it in most of the sessions that follow.

End of Session 8

- Review of problems and measures: at this stage in the programme it is a good idea to review the sessions thus far and re-administer the measures. Tell the young person that you have been monitoring the sessions through their feedback at the end of each meeting and this is an opportunity to look back at the original goals and reassess the level of distress to see how the therapy is going. Read out each problem and ask the young person to rate how bad it is now (out of 10). Do not show them the original ratings. If the problem has changed, then rewrite it in the same way as you did in Session 2. This will then be the focus for the following sessions. Also, repeat the standardised self-report measures you chose at the beginning (e.g. rating depressive mood (Mood and Feelings Questionnaire)(2) and self-esteem(3)).
- Homework: continue thought-challenging and, if appropriate, activity scheduling.
- Feedback.

Reference

1. Greenberger, D. and Padesky, C.A. (1995) *Mind over Mood: Change How You Feel by Changing the Way You Think*. New York: Guilford Press.
2. Costello, E.J. and Angold, A. (1988) Scales to assess child and adolescent depression: checklists, screens, and nets. *Journal of the American Academy of Child and Adolescent Psychiatry* 27, 726–737.
3. Rosenberg, M. (1965) *Society and the Adolescent Self-image*. Princeton, NJ: Princeton University Press.

HANDOUT FOR THE YOUNG PERSON: SESSION 8

Formulation

The formulation is how your 'story' fits together. In the previous sessions, you have focused on the individual parts that make up the formulation: the core beliefs, NATs and rules for living. The aim of formulation is to piece together how you have ended up being the person you are, and why you experience the world in the way that you do. It's a bit like making a map of your life. It can sometimes feel a bit uncomfortable to go back to the past and it can dredge up unpleasant memories, but it can also be a very helpful process to help us understand what makes you unique, to identify your 'danger spots' and to stop you falling into them over and over again.

The formulation comes from the theory that what we experience in our early lives (maybe even from when we are babies) is programmed into our minds and leads us to have certain beliefs about ourselves, the world, other people and the future. These implanted beliefs are designed to help us process information efficiently and make sense of a rapidly changing world. This is quite a good thing, as, for example, it would be very tiring (and a very inefficient use of our brains) if every time we looked at a chair, we had to relearn what it was and what it was used for.

However, if, for example, a young child feels scared when they are near certain people, they might start to believe that 'other people are dangerous', and this belief might then start to dictate their behaviour. Alternatively, if they start to believe that they are being compared unfavourably with a sibling who has different skills, they might start to believe that 'other people are more successful than me' or 'I'm no good'.

Thus, core beliefs are established when we are very young and continue to be established and strengthened as we grow up, and these can lead to certain rules of living that we follow, sometimes without even knowing that we are doing it. Sometimes, a specific event might 'activate' a core belief: for example, a person who feels 'unlovable' might become depressed when a relationship breaks down. This, in turn, will lead to an upsurge of NATs and behaviours that reinforce the core belief.

Coping strategies

This part is divided into ten modules. As before, depending on how easily the young person understands (or is already using) the concepts, aim to spend either one or two sessions on each module. The coping tree module itself is designed to help the young person choose the most suitable strategy. You might not need to spend a whole session on this, in which case it might be useful to combine another module with the description of the coping tree. Note that some of the basic coping strategies might have been used in earlier sessions. If this is the case, it is a good idea to review them and build on them as necessary.

Part Three: Cribsheet for the therapist

- Which strategies to use: the coping tree.
- Problem-solving.
- Assertiveness.
- Basic anger management.
- Taking care of yourself.
- Facing the situation.
- Riding the wave (managing emotions).
- Being mindful.
- Self-soothing.
- Coping highlights.
- Trouble-shooting: 'hot-spots'.

Aims of Part Three

The overall aim of this part is to enable the young person to explore a variety of coping strategies as alternatives to self-harm and to learn skills that help them manage difficult situations and emotions effectively. It is envisaged that by the time you reach this phase of therapy, you will have a fair idea of any relevant strategies for coping that the young person already utilises. You might also be aware of possible new strategies that might be beneficial for them to learn. This part teaches specific coping strategies and skills, and expands to consolidate and develop these skills further.

The modules are designed to be used and drawn on flexibly, depending on the needs of the young person. The techniques come from either Cognitive Behaviour Therapy or Dialectical Behaviour Therapy. Some are more directed towards 'change' strategies and others more towards 'acceptance'.(1) The change strategies are more akin to traditional CBT, based on a lack of skill or a specific problem area that needs teaching and alteration. The acceptance skills are designed to help the young person accept their circumstances at the time, with a view to changing problems when the distress levels have decreased.

Specific aims of the sessions

Session 9

- To decide which particular coping strategies are most appropriate for this young person. (Module 14)
- To introduce the concept of problem-solving, follow an example and start to utilise the young person's own examples to problem-solve. (Module 15)

Session 10

- To discuss three techniques that should help the young person to interact effectively and to manage their distress better. (Modules 16, 17 and 18)

Session 11

- To help the young person face their fears. (Module 19)

Session 12

- To introduce the 'mindfully aware' branch of the coping tree – the more acceptance-based strategies. (Modules 20, 21 and 22)

Session 13

- To consider alternatives to self-harm and pull together the various coping strategies that have been learned in earlier sessions. (Module 23)

Reference

1. Linehan, M. (1993) *Cognitive Behaviour Treatment of Borderline Personality Disorder*. New York: Guilford Press.

Session 9

This session comprises Modules 14 and 15. The principal aim is to use the coping tree to help the therapist and young person determine which coping strategies are most appropriate. The session then continues with the essential first skill: problem-solving.

Session 9: Cribsheet for the therapist

- Choosing which strategies to use: the coping tree.
- Problem-solving.

Module 14: The coping tree

Aims

The coping tree is designed to help you and the young person choose the most appropriate coping strategies. The literature strongly identifies depression (covered in the previous module), difficulties with problem-solving and emotional regulation as key areas to cover with young people who self-harm. For instance, with someone who struggles to tolerate strong feelings, you may choose to concentrate first on the 'mindfully aware' branches of the coping tree. Alternatively, if the young person has a lot of NATs and is feeling depressed, they may benefit more from the coping strategies in the feelings, thoughts and behaviours branches.

The coping tree does not need to be followed strictly; it is offered as a guide (see main session topic).

Agenda

- Bridge from last session.
- Homework review.
- Any issues raised by the young person (see earlier notes on this).
- Main session topic.

- Homework plan.
- Feedback.

Main session topic

Download Worksheet 36: The coping tree and see Figure 8.

Ask the young person to look at the tree and explain that you will talk them through the diagram. Tell them that this is a way of deciding which coping strategy to use when they are faced with a 'surge of emotion'. Explain that sometimes it is best to challenge negative thoughts immediately in order to alleviate feelings. However, on other occasions, it might be difficult to identify such thoughts or quicker and easier to accept a thought/emotion and let it go for the time being, with a view to dealing with the problem later, when they are feeling less emotionally aroused.

Explain to the young person that they can use the coping tree whenever they notice a strong feeling on their feelings scale (5 or more). Starting from the bottom, they should 'go up' the roots of the tree to make a decision about the best course of action – which coping strategy to use. At this point, the young person needs to take a step back from the situation and analyse what is going on – what is happening in their environment and what is happening in their head and body, as measured through their thoughts and emotions. You might want to help them pick a recent emotionally loaded event and try this out.

THE COPING TREE: CASSIE

Cassie described an intense feeling of emptiness and loneliness when her friend did not call around to help her with her homework. She rated this a 6 on the feelings scale. Using the coping tree as a guide, she was able to separate herself from the situation that had triggered her emotion.

She reflected on the way she handled the situation in terms of her immediate thoughts and behaviours. For instance, one automatic thought that came into her head was: 'Everyone always lets me down; no one is there for me.' Her physical response was to cry and she described how her body felt numb. To alleviate her feeling of 'emptiness', she cut the top of her leg with a razor.

Reviewing the situation, Cassie was able to come up with several thoughts to challenge her original negative, dysfunctional, ones. For example, she was able to think of times when her family and friends *had* come to her aid and helped her with various tasks. She was also able to look at the situation from her friend's perspective and remembered that her friend had been very busy and had simply forgotten to call. There was no reason to think that her friend did not like her.

Another coping mechanism might have been for Cassie to let go of her negative thought and try to distract herself with her homework until the feelings subsided.

After they have figured out what is going on, the young person can move up the tree trunk, where they have two primary options. They can move

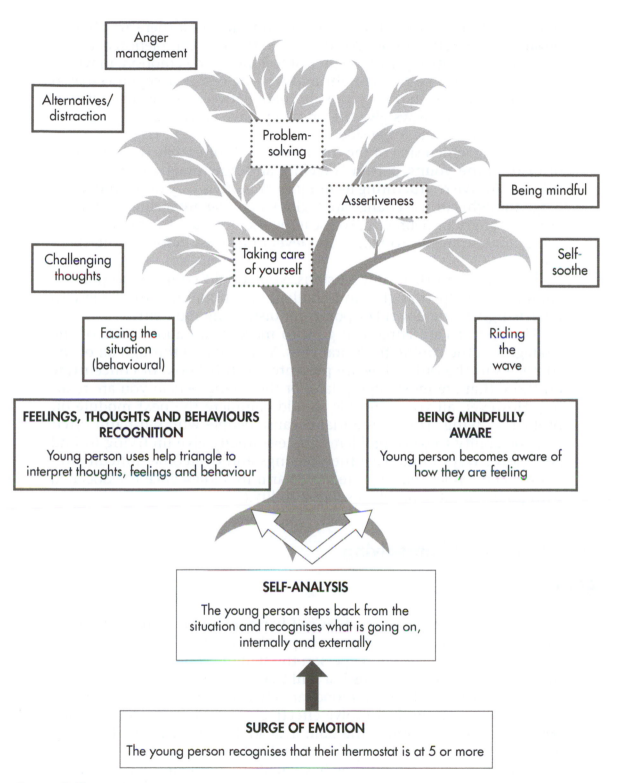

Figure 8 The coping tree

to the left and try one of the change-based strategies if there are obvious negative interpretations or NATs (identified through completion of a help triangle). Alternatively, they might just feel the strong emotion, in which case they should go to the right and try one of the acceptance-based strategies. Explain that they can alternate between these two options, but they should always give the one they have chosen a full go before moving across to the other side.

Deciding which side of the tree to choose is often based on the level of distress the young person is feeling and how practised they are at using cognitive restructuring techniques. It is often very difficult to challenge thoughts or use change strategies when you are feeling extremely anxious, angry or depressed, so it can be useful to use the mindfulness/ acceptance strategies to reduce the level of distress before trying them out.

During the forthcoming sessions, you should continue to practise completing help triangles and challenging thoughts with a view to rehearsing/writing down key points for distressing moments.

The rest of Part Three will go into more detail about each of the strategies in the coping tree's branches. You could go through all of the strategies in the order they are presented in this book, or concentrate on those that are most appropriate for the young person you are treating. However, all young people should complete the next module on problem-solving. This is essential because people who self-harm often lose the ability to solve problems and eventually give up trying to find alternative ways to manage their feelings and overcome difficult situations. Remember that repeated self-harm in adolescence is associated with poor self-rated problem-solving ability.(1)

Module 15: Problem-solving

Aims

Dysfunctional behaviours such as self-harm are often seen as problems to be solved, or as faulty solutions to problems in life.(2) The aim of this module is to teach the young person the skill of problem-solving and to help them recognise that this is a skill that we all need.

Feeling depressed, low in mood, anxious or under-confident can disable our ability to problem-solve effectively. Furthermore, some young people have *never* acquired the skill; instead, they have learned to manage their distress through dysfunctional behaviour, such as self-harm. Alternatively, any attempts they have made to problem-solve might not have been reinforced, or might even have been punished by their environment. For instance, a teenage girl who is struggling at school might suggest moving to a less academically orientated establishment. Instead of thinking this through and supporting her proposal, her parents might get angry and forbid the move because they cannot understand why their daughter would want to leave a 'good school'. Although they might not intend to be punitive, their behaviour does not show any understanding of or support for their daughter's attempt to try to solve a difficult problem.

The main aim of this module is to enable the young person to generate alternative strategies to self-harm. Tell them that hassles and problems are aspects of everyday life for everyone. Parents, friends, boy/girlfriends, school, work – almost anything – can create problems in our lives at one time or another. Luckily, we are usually quite good at coping with many of these problems and are able to address them quickly and successfully.

However, other problems can be more difficult to resolve. This might be because:

- They happen fairly often.
- They have been around for some time.
- They feel totally overwhelming (this can happen with either one big problem or lots of smaller problems).
- They seem to affect everything you do.
- They occur in a context of high emotional arousal.

Sometimes these problems take over and life becomes one big worry. At other times, when you try to solve them, you only make matters worse, or you fail to achieve the effect you want, or every potential solution seems to have a downside. Consequently, you feel stuck.

Problem-solving can be as simple as deciding what to have for breakfast, or it can be as complicated as choosing which A-levels to take, or working out how to patch things up with a good friend after an argument. However, in every case it is important to tackle problems rather than avoid them (even if we don't even want to think about them); otherwise, we can be overwhelmed by feelings or by trying to find the 'perfect' solution. Some problems can escalate if left unattended for too long; or, if the problem is interpersonal, the other person might get fed up and lose patience.

Problem-solving involves breaking down a worry or an issue into a specific problem, analysing that problem to generate possible solutions, then attempting to fix it, if indeed it is fixable. It is no good worrying constantly about world hunger as that is not a problem we can fix. However, it is possible to fix the problem of worrying constantly. This can be done by defining the potentially *solvable* problem (worry), generating several possible solutions, highlighting the pros and cons of each, then testing them out in turn, starting with the most plausible.

Exercise: Problem-solving

Download Worksheet 37: Problem-solving and go through Katy's and Jessica's examples. Ask the young person at each step what they might do if they were in a similar situation.

> **PROBLEM-SOLVING: KATY**
>
> 'I don't know what to do. It's awful! It happened yesterday! What happened was I was on the bus with my so-called mate Shelley and we were talking about my other mate Lennie. I only said he was nice! But she got totally the wrong end of the stick and I arrived at school this morning and everyone's talking behind my back! Lennie's girlfriend is giving me evil looks and I'm scared she's gonna hit me. Everyone's laughing at me! I can't ever go back to school!'

> **PROBLEM-SOLVING: JESSICA**
>
> 'This always happens! I'm sick of his stupid rules, he makes my mum do what he thinks and he doesn't even live at home! Why can't he just leave me alone and let me have a life?! This time it is about this gig that everyone is going to! It's so stupid. I'm not allowed to go because apparently it finishes "too late for a school night". Who does he think he is? He has never cared about me before!'

Step 1: Identify the problem

How is Katy going to deal with her friend, Lennie and the other people at school?

Step 2: List every possible solution

1. Never go to school again.
2. Send Shelley a nasty email.
3. Arrange a fight with Lennie's girlfriend.
4. Kiss Lennie.
5. Ignore people laughing.
6. Go home, cry and take some tablets.
7. Confront Shelley and try to sort it out.
8. Talk to Lennie and his girlfriend about what really happened.
9. Ask another friend to talk to Lennie.
10. Tell a teacher.

Step 3: Assess each possible solution

For example, for possible solution 1: Never go to school again:

- Pros: I don't need to feel embarrassed; I don't like school anyway.
- Cons: my dad would kill me; I won't get any GCSEs or get into college; they'll think they've 'won' and I'll feel weak; I'll lose all my friends.

Step 4: Choose the best solution or combination of solutions

Solutions to try following after assessing all possible solutions in Step 3 (in order, with best option first):

- 8: Talk to Lennie and his girlfriend because, although it won't be easy, there are more pros than cons for this option.
- 5: Ignore the laughing because I don't want them to feel they've won!

Step 5: Plan how to carry out the best solution

- Jot down what I want to say so it's clear in my head.
- Plan a good time to catch Lennie with his girlfriend on their own (after English).
- Let them know that I want to *talk* to them, not fight.
- Explain the situation that I only like him as a friend and I'm not trying to steal him from her! Shelley got it all wrong.
- Make sure I've got my friend to talk to afterwards.

Step 6: Review how it's going

- What obstacles might get in the way?
- How might you deal with them?
- What is your plan B?

This could work and the problem will be solved, which would be great. But if it fails, remember Katy has lots of other options to try.

FINDING A SOLUTION THAT WORKS: KATY

'I tried really hard to find them on their own, but there were always loads of people with them and I just couldn't do it in front of everyone else. So I wrote them a note instead and it's all OK again now.'

Now ask the young person to come up with their own example and go through the six steps with them:

1. Identify the problem.
2. List every possible solution. (Be as open-minded and creative as possible with potential solutions. It doesn't matter how extreme they are. The idea is to get the young person thinking.)
3. Discuss the pros and cons of each possible solution.
4. Choose the best solution or combination of solutions. (This might be the one with the most pros and the fewest cons, or it could simply be the one that the young person is willing to try.)

5. Plan how to carry out the best solution.
6. Review how it's going:

- What obstacles might get in the way?
- How might you deal with them?
- What is your plan B?

Remember, if the first solution doesn't work, you can always go back to Step 4 and try a different one.

End of Session 9

- Homework: identify a problem and go through the six steps; or, if this was done in the session, try out the agreed solution during the week.
- Feedback.

Reference

1. Hawton, K., Salkovskis, P.M., Kirk, J. and Clark D.M. (1989) *Cognitive Behaviour Therapy for Psychiatric Problems: A Practical Guide.* Oxford: Oxford Medical Publications.
2. Linehan, M. (1993) *Cognitive Behaviour Treatment of Borderline Personality Disorder.* New York: Guilford Press.

HANDOUT FOR THE YOUNG PERSON: SESSION 9 (a)

The coping tree – which strategy should I use?

The coping tree is a way of deciding which coping strategy you should use when you are faced with a 'surge of emotion'. Sometimes it might be most useful to challenge negative thoughts to reduce intense feelings. At other times, it might be difficult to identify the thoughts or it might be quicker and easier to accept a thought/emotion and let it go, with a view to dealing with the problem when you are less emotionally aroused.

The bottom of the tree is the place to start. This is when you first notice a strong feeling (a rating of 5 or more on your feelings scale). When you have noticed the feeling, 'go up' the roots of the tree and make a decision as to the best course of action – which coping strategy to use. At this point, you should try to take a step back from the situation and analyse what is going on. Think about what is happening around you and what is happening in your mind and body. Focus on your thoughts and emotions.

After figuring out what is going on, move up the tree trunk. Now you have two alternatives. You could try one of the change-based strategies if you know you have put a negative spin on the situation or you have noticed any NATs; use a help triangle. Alternatively, you might just feel the strong emotion, and have no obvious thoughts, in which case you might want to move to the right-hand side of the tree and try an acceptance-based strategy. You can alternate between these two options and your therapist will explain more about them and run through some examples with you in future sessions. If you do alternate, you must try to give the strategy you picked first a good go, before moving to the other side.

Remember, it is often very difficult to challenge thoughts or use change strategies when you are feeling extremely anxious, angry or depressed. So it can be useful to use one of the mindfulness/acceptance strategies first, to reduce the levels of distress. Then, when you are feeling calmer, employ one of the change strategies.

HANDOUT FOR THE YOUNG PERSON: SESSION 9 (b)

Problem-solving

Self-harm can often make it difficult to find alternative ways to solve problems. The main aim of this module is to help you generate those alternatives for yourself.

Hassles and problems are aspects of everyday life. Parents, friends, boy/girl-friends, school, work – almost anything – can create problems in our lives at one time or another. Luckily, we are usually quite good at coping with many of these problems and are able to address them quickly and successfully.

However, other problems can seem more difficult to resolve. This may be because:

- They happen fairly often.
- They have been around for some time.
- They feel totally overwhelming (this can happen with one big problem or lots of smaller problems).
- They seem to affect everything you do.
- They occur in a context of high emotional arousal.

Sometimes these problems take over and life becomes one big worry. At other times, when you try to solve them, you only make matters worse, or you fail to achieve the effect you want, or every potential solution seems to have a downside. Consequently, you feel stuck. Problem-solving can be as simple as deciding what to have for breakfast, or it can be as complicated as choosing which A-levels to take, or working out how to patch things up with a good friend after an argument. However, in every case it is important to tackle problems rather than avoid them (even if we don't even want to think about them); otherwise, we can be overwhelmed by feelings or by trying to find the 'perfect' solution. Some problems can escalate if left unattended for too long; or, if the problem is interpersonal, the other person might get fed up and lose patience.

Problem-solving involves breaking down a worry or an issue into a specific problem, analysing that problem to generate possible solutions, then attempting to fix it, if indeed it is fixable. It is no good worrying constantly about world hunger as that is not a problem we can fix. However, it is possible to fix the problem of worrying constantly. This can be done by defining the *solvable* problem (worry), generating several possible solutions, highlighting the pros and cons of each, then testing them out in turn, starting with the most plausible.

There are six basic steps to problem-solving:

1. Identify the problem.
2. List every possible solution. (Be as open-minded and creative as possible with potential solutions. It doesn't matter how extreme they seem.)
3. Discuss the pros and cons of each possible solution.

4. Choose the best solution or combination of solutions. (This might be the one with the most pros and the fewest cons, or it could simply be the one that you are willing to try.)
5. Plan how to carry out the best solution.
6. Review how it's going:

- What obstacles might get in the way?
- How might you deal with them?
- What is your plan B?

Remember, if the first solution doesn't work, you can always go back to Step 4 and try a different one.

Session 10

This session comprises Modules 16 and 17 and 18, as required. If you are working through all the modules, these modules can be delivered in two sessions. Three core skills are addressed. The first two are interpersonal skills – assertiveness and anger management. Following this, we present a strategy that is designed to help young people become less self-critical and learn how to look after themselves.

Session 10: Cribsheet for the therapist

- Interpersonal skill – assertiveness.
- Interpersonal skill – anger management.
- Taking care of yourself – dealing with self-criticism.

Module 16: Assertiveness

When people get caught with not asserting their needs and being extremely self-critical, their self-esteem declines and self-harm can become a strategy to manage these difficult feelings.

Agenda

- Bridge from last session.
- Homework review: problem-solving homework. Go through this together, identifying any difficulties and issues that arose.
- Any issues raised by the young person (see earlier notes on this).
- Main session topic.
- Homework plan.
- Feedback.

Aim

The aim of this section is to enable the young person to assert their needs, desires, wishes and feelings effectively.

Main session topic

Assertiveness is an essential skill that is required for healthy and productive relationships. Problems are encountered when issues arise between people and when the immediate behaviours used are either passive or aggressive in nature.(1) Possessing the ability to behave assertively can help avoid any feelings of pent-up frustration, which can often result when a person ends up doing things they do not want to do, leading to feelings of regret, self-disgust and, ultimately, self-harm.

The first key skills in being assertive are saying what you really feel and negotiating what you want. Ask the young person: 'Do you sometimes find yourself going along with something when you don't really want to, and then feeling angry or upset with people afterwards?' If they relate to this feeling, continue with the discussion. (Bear in mind that some young people might struggle with the opposite problem – getting angry and aggressive when pressure is placed on them. However, even if this is the case, further discussion of assertiveness should be useful.)

Tell the young person that it's not always easy to say 'no' to someone, especially a friend, and explain that this can be particularly difficult when we want to fit in and don't want to stand out as being different. Many people worry that they won't be liked if they say what they really feel. The idea of not being liked is pretty horrible, so there is pressure to do things we don't really want to do, including: revealing intimate details about our lives; taking drugs; skipping school; or going to a party or club.

However, *always* going along with others and trying to please them usually leads you to feel worse about yourself and reduces the respect other people have for you. Standing up for your rights or having a different opinion means that it is sometimes essential to say 'no'. There are various ways to do this. For example, it can be done aggressively, by shouting at or threatening the other person, but this is usually ineffective, because it just makes the other person angry and can lead to arguments. Alternatively, saying 'no' can be done in an assertive way: you stand up for yourself in a calm manner, while continuing to respect the other person's feelings and wishes. This usually works very well, but a lot of young people (and many adults!) find it very hard to do.

Exercise: Asserting yourself

Download Worksheet 38: Assertiveness. Look together at Cassie's options for dealing with her difficult situation and ask the young person if they can remember times when they have felt under similar pressure. Then discuss the possible consequences of submitting to peer pressure.

CASSIE'S SITUATION

'Although it was a huge effort, I did go to my friend's party but when we left my friends decided to go on to another house party. I didn't want to because I felt too drunk and miserable, and I just wanted to go home.'

CASSIE'S OPTIONS

- The 'pleasing others' response: 'I ended up going and hated it! Then I got into a lot of trouble as I had to get my step-dad to pick me up. I felt so crap that I went home and cut my arm really badly. I wish I'd stuck to what I wanted to do.'
- The aggressive response: 'None of them appreciated that I'd come out when I didn't want to and said I was selfish because I wanted to go home. I went mad and told them all to f*** off. When they left I threw my bottle after them. The neighbour called the police and now I've lost *all* my friends!'
- The assertive response: 'I really didn't want to go, so I said I was really tired and that I'd had enough. They were disappointed and tried to persuade me but I didn't budge. Eventually my friend Sally said she was tired too and she'd come with me. We had a really good chat on the way home.'

Exercise: Assertiveness role-play

Now, using the blank boxes after Cassie's potential responses in Worksheet 38, you can explore what the young person might have done in a similar situation. They should choose a real-life situation when they wanted to say something but ended up going along with the group, even though they did not want to. (If they are unable to come up with an example, use Cassie's.)

- Scenario 1: The young person acts as himself/herself (non-assertive) and the therapist plays the role of friend/other.
- Scenario 2: Discuss what the young person wishes they had said, or what they imagine an 'assertive person' might have said. Play around with various ideas: for example, someone they think is cool, a strong fictional character, someone in their class, a family member, etc. Using the identified strategies, the young person should play the 'assertive person' while the therapist gives feedback on what it feels like to be face to face with such a person.
- Scenario 3: Swap, so that the young person starts to learn how it feels to be on the other end of assertiveness. Encourage a discussion to dispel their beliefs that being assertive will result in a loss of friends and help them see that it is more likely to encourage respect.

Role-play provides an opportunity to modify plans if the young person feels they will not work.

Exercise: How do you become assertive?

Training in assertiveness involves helping the young person to develop social behaviours to cope with pressure. This is best achieved by planning, rehearsing and practising refusal behaviours.

Still using Worksheet 38, go through the following three steps with the young person.

Step 1: Preparation

- What I want to say: Describe the situation or the problem that is important to you, rather than focusing on the other person or their actions. Try to be as specific as possible: for example, 'I am thinking that you all want to go to the other party.'
- My feelings: Say how you feel about the situation or problem: for example, 'I am sorry/sad I won't be able to go with you to the party.'
- My needs: Say what you want to happen to make things different: for example, 'I need to go home to go to bed.'
- The outcome: Being assertive and behaving in a certain way will improve the situation for you *and* for the other person: for example, 'If you all go to the party and I go home, we will all be happier.'

Step 2: Strategies

Download Worksheet 39: BEST skill – an acronym to help the young person to remember the basics when they need to be assertive in real-life situations:

- **B**e clear – state what the situation is.
- **E**xpress your feelings – use 'I . . .' statements, not 'You make me feel . . .' statements.
- **S**ay what you want calmly and simply.
- **T**ry to negotiate if it is not working, or if you meet with resistance.

Once the young person is familiar with this basic guide, they can explore more skills. Go through them together and ask the young person to think about situations when such strategies might be useful (Worksheet 38).

- Broken record: When you want to stick to your guns, try imagining you are an old style vinyl record that has got stuck, or a CD that is scratched, saying 'no' or expressing your opinion over and over again. No matter what the other person says or does, just keep repeating the same point.

- Script it: Write down what you want to say beforehand and rehearse it.
- Ignore: If you are feeling pressurised in any way, try ignoring what the other person is saying or doing. This can be really hard to do, but it sends out a powerful message!
- Turn the tables: Turn the problem over to the other person. Ask them to think of something you can do together, but don't agree to do anything that is unappealing: for example, 'I can't say "yes" to that, even though you want me to. What can we do about it?'
- Act cool: Concentrate on acting confident, even if you don't feel it. Imagine how a friend or someone you admire might behave in the situation and try to act in the same way.
- Give to get: Sometimes you have to 'give to get'. Without forgetting about what you want, try to find a way to meet the other person half-way. See if there is something else you can offer while maintaining your 'no'. Maybe reduce your demand to something that can be fulfilled.

WHAT HAPPENED WHEN CASSIE USED AN ASSERTIVE STRATEGY

'My friend wanted me to bunk off English with her as she hadn't done her homework. I knew she was really worried about it and I didn't want to let her down, but at the same time English is my favourite lesson! It's the only one I really enjoy at the moment, as we are writing poetry, and I really didn't want to miss it. She said I was selfish if I went to the lesson, as then she would have to go too. I decided to try being a "broken record". I told her I knew she was worried about her homework but I wasn't going to bunk off the lesson with her. She tried really hard to convince me but I just kept saying, "No. I like English. I'm not bunking off." I felt stronger every time I said it! After a while she accepted it and we talked about what excuses she could give for not doing her homework.'

Step 3: Practise

Being assertive is not always easy, and the best way to build confidence is through practice. Ask the young person to think of situations in their day-to-day life where they could practise being assertive. (Remind them that it might be easier to start small.) If nothing comes to mind, you could suggest the following examples (see Worksheet 38):

- Go to a shop and ask where something is (e.g. in a supermarket, ask for the shampoo).
- While talking with someone, change the subject to something you want to talk about.
- Ask for no sauce/a different topping in a fast-food restaurant.
- Ask for the bill when you're out for a meal with a friend.
- Ring a private gym and ask if you can attend a class and pay separately.
- Invite a friend out to the cinema/shopping.

- Go into a shop and ask for change for the bus.
- Ask a friend to do you a favour.
- Disagree with someone's opinion (e.g. say that you don't like *EastEnders*).
- Send back a meal in a restaurant because it is too cold/too small for the price.
- Give someone a compliment/accept a compliment by saying 'Thank you'.

The next skill you will be discussing with the young person is a continuation of the skills that enable them to respect their own needs while also getting along with other people. They will have a clear idea about the link between their thoughts and emotions and in particular about any negative thoughts they have about themselves.

Module 17: Basic anger management

Aims

Many young people who self-harm complain of problems with controlling their anger. This module is not intended to be an exhaustive anger management training programme. Rather, its aim is simply to help the young person recognise if anger is an issue for them, and then to offer some skills that will help them understand and cope when their anger is getting out of control.

Main session topic

If it has not already come up as an issue, ask the young person if they have ever got into trouble because of their anger, or if it has wrecked a specific situation for them. If they say that this is not a problem for them, you can move on to Module 18. However, if they admit that they have had trouble with their anger, stick with this module. Explain that anger is not a problem per se (look back at the exercise 'Feelings are our friends'). A problem arises only if anger impacts negatively on relationships or impairs the young person's functioning in another way. For example, see Mark's anger scale (Figure 9). His anger can get out of control at times and he has been suspended from school for hitting another pupil in front of a teacher.

After looking at Mark's example, tell the young person that the first step in anger management is to learn how to become aware of the stages of anger as it develops. Then it will be possible to escape from the situation by using adaptive interpersonal skills (e.g. assertiveness; or mindfulness, then distraction) *before* the anger gets out of control.

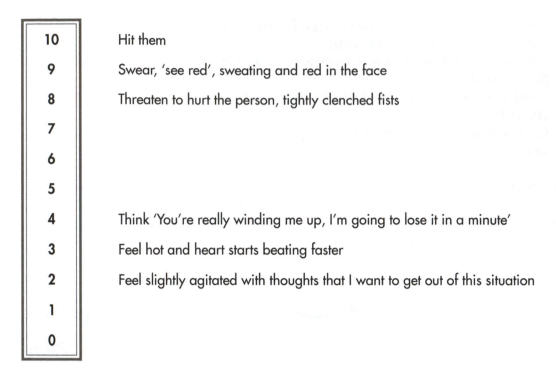

10	Hit them
9	Swear, 'see red', sweating and red in the face
8	Threaten to hurt the person, tightly clenched fists
7	
6	
5	
4	Think 'You're really winding me up, I'm going to lose it in a minute'
3	Feel hot and heart starts beating faster
2	Feel slightly agitated with thoughts that I want to get out of this situation
1	
0	

Figure 9 Mark's anger scale

Exercise: My anger scale

Download Worksheet 40: My anger scale and ask the young person to rate how quickly they move from a 1 to a 10 when they are angry. Write the stages of anger next to the relevant positions on the scale to identify what happens as the anger escalates. When you do this exercise with the young person, try to identify their physical sensations at the various stages, as well as their thoughts and any actions or predicted actions. The more sensations, feelings, thoughts and actions they can identify at each stage, the easier it will be to stop the process early.

Exercise: Imagination task

Ask the young person to think about the last time they got extremely angry and completely 'lost it'. Then tell them to imagine reaching 2 or 3 on the anger scale. State the signs that correlate with this stage which the young person identified in the previous exercise. Then get them to imagine employing a coping strategy (e.g. walking away or being assertive, as appropriate). Practise imagining the triggers for the anger (e.g. someone winding them up) but remaining calm. This exercise needs to be practised every day, so it would be useful to schedule it as a homework task for this session.

If you have gone through this module with the young person, Module 18 might now prove useful in helping them to relax and calm down.

Module 18: Taking care of yourself

Aims

This module will highlight self-critical thoughts, continue to challenge self-harming young people's negative thoughts and help them to find alternative, more positive ways of viewing themselves.

Exercise: Self-description

Ask the young person to make a list of at least ten words or phrases that best describe them. Prompt for at least two positive words or phrases (you can use the strengths sheet – Worksheet 14 – to remind them of the positive qualities they have already identified) but allow them to provide some negative characteristics too, if they wish. This can be validating to their feelings of low self-esteem and negativity at this point.

Exercise: Challenging self-critical thoughts

Explain that sometimes the words that we feel best describe ourselves are also self-critical thoughts. Ask the young person to write down their self-critical thoughts (for example, 'I am useless') and prompt them to think about the similarities between those thoughts and the words and phrases they have just listed in the self-description exercise. Remind them of Module 10, when they identified and challenged their negative automatic thoughts.

Download Worksheet 41: Help with challenging your thoughts, which should help the young person to think about their self-critical thoughts and find alternatives.

JESSICA'S SELF-CRITICAL THOUGHTS

'I'm unlovable . . . moody . . . fat . . .'

Jessica looked back at her thought record and saw her previous evidence for and against one of her NATs: moodiness. Then she wrote down some alternatives and looked for evidence over the course of the next week.

Previous evidence:

- Sometimes I get moody, but so does everyone . . . and I'm happy a lot of the time.
- It's good that I can show my feelings.
- When I feel bad that I'm moody, I should just check out if that's how I really come across.

continued

Alternatives:

- My mate Sonia said she wishes she could be more like me and let people know she felt crap and didn't feel like mucking around that day.
- My support worker said what a good week I'd had and how lovely it was to be around me . . . but I had thought I had been a right moody cow!

Continue with the NAT work, including the work from the earlier module (Module 10). The aim is to expand the cognitive restructuring skills of the young person, so that it becomes an extremely practised skill. This can extend into the next session, if necessary: for example, if the young person is particularly depressed or describes regular and distressing NATs. Remember to use the thought record and appropriate worksheets from the previous module.

At this point, if the young person has low self-esteem and is highly self-critical, there is the option of focusing a bit more on raising their self-esteem, using Homework for Module 18 (b). Remind them of the strengths sheet they completed earlier (Worksheet 14).

End of Session 10

- Homework for Module 16: the young person should plan how to respond to a potential 'assertiveness' situation and think about which strategies to try. It's fine to start with something small, such as asking for change in a shop.
- Homework for Module 17: using the anger scale, the young person should practise avoiding the 'blow-up' of reaching 10 in a potentially angry situation. They should use skills and strategies as appropriate, including assertiveness, walking away and thought-challenging.
- Homework for Module 18 (a): ask the young person to choose three alternative thoughts that challenge their self-critical thoughts. Then ask them to write down any evidence that supports these new thoughts over the course of the next week. (This could be something they do, something someone says to them, and so on.) See Jessica's example, above.
- Homework for Module 18 (b): the young person should focus on one or two of the strengths identified in Worksheet 14 and jot down any time something happens that provides supporting evidence for that strength: for example, if a friend says they are a good listener, they should write down a time when they listened to someone during the week. This may have been practised already, but it is beneficial to repeat it.
- Feedback.

Reference

1. McKay, M., Wood, J.C. and Brantley, J. (2007) *The Dialectical Behavior Therapy Skills Workbook: Practical DBT Exercises for Learning Mindfulness, Interpersonal Effectiveness, Emotion Regulation, and Distress Tolerance.* Oakland, CA: New Harbinger Publications.

HANDOUT FOR THE YOUNG PERSON: SESSION 10 (a)

What is assertiveness?

The ability to assert your needs, desires, wishes and feelings effectively. It means that you can stand up for yourself in a calm manner, while at the same time being mindful of the other person's feelings and wishes. This way can work very well, but a lot of young people (and many adults) find it very hard to do.

Assertiveness is an essential skill for healthy relationships. Problems are encountered when issues arise between people and when people are either passive or aggressive towards the other person. The ability to behave assertively can help avoid any feelings of pent-up frustration, which can often lead to a person doing things they do not want to do, leading to feelings of regret, self-disgust and, ultimately, self-harm.

The first key skill in assertiveness is saying what you really feel and negotiating for what you really want.

- Do you sometimes find yourself going along with something when you don't really want to, and then feeling angry or upset with people afterwards?
- Do you sometimes find that you get extremely angry or aggressive when people ask you to do stuff or put pressure on you?

It is not always easy to say 'no' to someone, especially a friend, particularly when you want to fit in and don't want to seem different. You might worry that people won't like you if you say what you really feel. The idea of not being liked is pretty horrible, so you could feel under pressure to do things you don't really want to do, such as revealing intimate details about yourself, taking drugs, skipping school or going to a club.

When you think about it, *always* going along with others and trying to please them usually ends up with you feeling worse and other people respecting you less. Standing up for your rights or having different opinions means that sometimes you must say 'no'.

Steps to being assertive

Step 1: Preparation

- What I want to say: Describe the situation or the problem that is important to you, rather than focusing on the other person or their actions. Try to be as specific as possible: for example, 'I am thinking that you all want to go to the other party.'
- My feelings: Say how you feel about the situation or problem: for example, 'I am sorry/sad I won't be able to go with you to the party.'
- My needs: Say what you want to happen to make things different: for example, 'I need to go home to go to bed.'

- The outcome: Being assertive and behaving in a certain way will improve the situation for you *and* for the other person: for example, 'If you all go to the party and I go home, we will all be happier.'

Step 2: Strategies

- BEST.
- Broken record: When you want to stick to your guns, try imagining you are an old style vinyl record that has got stuck, or a CD that is scratched, saying 'no' or expressing your opinion over and over again. No matter what the other person says or does, just keep repeating the same point.
- Script it: Write down what you want to say beforehand and rehearse it.
- Ignore: If you are feeling pressurised in any way, try ignoring what the other person is saying or doing. This can be really hard to do, but it sends out a powerful message!
- Turn the tables: Turn the problem over to the other person. Ask them to think of something you can do together, but don't agree to do anything that is unappealing: for example, 'I can't say "yes" to that, even though you want me to. What can we do about it?'
- Act cool: Concentrate on acting confident, even if you don't feel it. Imagine how a friend or someone you admire might behave in the situation and try to act in the same way.
- Give to get: Sometimes you have to 'give to get'. Without forgetting about what you want, try to find a way to meet the other person half way. See if there is something else you can offer while maintaining your 'no'. Maybe reduce your demand to something that can be fulfilled.

Step 3: Practise, practise, practise!

HANDOUT FOR THE YOUNG PERSON: SESSION 10 (b)

Anger management

Have you ever got into trouble because of your anger or has it wrecked a situation for you?

Note that feeling angry isn't a problem in itself (remember: emotions are our friends). The problem arises only if anger impacts negatively on your relationships or affects your day-to-day life in some way.

Try to identify all the different sensations you feel at each stage on the anger scale. Also, try to think about all the thoughts, actions or predicted actions. This will help you to stop the process earlier, before the anger escalates too far.

HANDOUT FOR THE YOUNG PERSON: SESSION 10 (c)

Taking care of yourself

You need to explore your self-critical thinking and get really good at challenging your negative thoughts. The aim is to try to find alternative, more positive ways of viewing yourself.

People who self-harm often think very badly about themselves and have low self-esteem.

- Challenge your self-critical thoughts: Sometimes the words that we feel describe us well are also self-critical thoughts.
- Strengths and developing self-esteem: Look back over Worksheet 14, where you identified your strengths, and remind yourself of the things you are good at and what other people like about you.

Session 11

This session aims to address specific anxieties, in particular avoidance.

Session 11: Cribsheet for the therapist

- Treating anxiety and avoidance.
- Developing a hierarchy and exposure.

Module 19: Facing the situation

Aim

This module focuses on addressing anxiety through exposure and desen-sitisation to the anxious feeling. The aim is to activate the young person behaviourally to face avoidance and/or increase activities.

Agenda

- Bridge from last session.
- Homework review. Review the four possible homework options from the previous session, address any issues and reinforce any successful attempts to try out the strategies.
- Any issues raised by the young person (see earlier notes on this).
- Main session topic.
- Homework plan.
- Feedback.

Main session topic

Anxiety and avoidance can play key roles in the feeling of distress in young people who self-harm. The anxiety may be about specific situa-tions in social areas, separation or change. In CBT, anxiety is broken into three parts: thoughts, physical sensations and behaviours that help the person avoid the feared situations. General treatment for anxiety focuses on specific maintaining factors and includes psycho-education about anxiety, exposure to feared stimuli, relaxation skills, cognitive restructuring, reward systems and role-play.

If the young person has stopped performing certain activities, is very depressed or is very anxious and avoiding situations, this session should help them develop strategies that allow them to face the feared situations.

If the young person remains depressed, you might continue with more activity scheduling, introducing some novel activities.

Exercise: The facing my fears ladder

Download Worksheet 42: Facing my fears ladder. If the young person is anxious and so avoiding situations, start to build up their ladder on Worksheet 42. Explain that in order to overcome anxiety, people must allow themselves to be exposed to the feared situations until the anxiety subsides. A useful way to start this process is to place the frightening situations in a hierarchy – or ladder – of about ten increasingly threatening stimuli (the rungs of the ladder). For example, if the young person is socially anxious and feels that going to a party would cause them extreme anxiety (10 out of 10), this would be placed at the top of the ladder. On the lower rungs would be less anxiety-inducing situations, such as going for a coffee with a good friend (say, 3 out of 10, so the third rung).

KATY'S FEAR LADDER

Katy feared going back to school following an embarrassing incident among her peers. Her goal was to 'return to school'. She was invited by her therapist to build a fear ladder. First, she listed the situations, places and things that she feared. Then she ranked them from least scary to most scary:

- Walking to school in the morning.
- Meeting other classmates.
- Going to class.
- Lunchtime in the canteen.
- Meeting Lennie.
- Bumping into Lennie's girlfriend.

Following a discussion of Katy's example, tell the young person that it is now time for them to identify a hierarchy of their specific anxiety-provoking situations, using Worksheet 9: The feelings scale. It can be useful to ask the young person what they would like to get out of this exercise. (The primary goal should be to improve their quality of life and not to be forced to do unwelcome things.)

Suggest possibilities for the different rungs, but make sure that the ladder remains specific to the young person. It is useful to include a couple of examples at each rung: for instance, going for coffee with a good friend and taking the bus round the block might both be rated as 3 out of 10. Having different examples on the same rung means you have a choice if it is not possible to set up some exposure experiments. Also, the young person will be able to get on with several exposure challenges during a single week, which will speed up their habituation to anxiety. Each situation should be practised several times.

Let the young person know that they are in control of each rung of the hierarchy. They should not move up to the next situation until the anxiety level of the one they are addressing has decreased to 2 or less (pre-agree this rating).

In some circumstances, situations can be practised with the therapist, during the session. Make sure you identify any cognitions associated with entering the situation and any negative predictions that can be challenged. Rate the anxiety level as the young person enters the situation, during it and afterwards. Do not leave the situation until the anxiety has subsided.

End of Session 11

- Homework: the young person should practise going into anxiety-inducing situations repeatedly.
- Feedback.

HANDOUT FOR THE YOUNG PERSON: SESSION 11

Anxiety and avoidance

Anxiety and avoidance can play key roles in the feeling of distress in young people who self-harm. The anxiety may be about specific situations in social areas, separation or change. In CBT, anxiety is broken into three parts: thoughts, physical sensations and behaviours that help the person avoid feared situations. General treatment for anxiety focuses on specific factors that maintain the problem. It also addresses education about anxiety, facing your fears, relaxation skills, managing unhelpful thoughts, reward strategies that speed up the process and role-play, or practising tricky scenarios.

If you are avoiding situations because you are anxious, you and your therapist will develop a ladder of difficult situations. In order to overcome the anxiety, you will work your way up the ladder to face your fears (with support from your therapist, using anxiety management skills and remembering that you are always in control of when you take the next step). Your quality of life should improve as you practise this exercise and it will give you the strength to resist doing unwelcome things. Remember to practise each situation over and over again, to rate your level of anxiety at the beginning, middle and end of each situation, and to stay there until your anxiety has decreased significantly.

Session 12

This session is comprised of three modules: Module 20: Riding the wave; Module 21: Being mindful; and Module 22: Self-soothing. All three modules are based on acceptance strategies on the right-hand side of the coping tree. Until now, we have focused on CBT change strategies, so that the young person has the skills to manage their emotions and effect change in their thoughts, behaviours and emotions. However, there are times when it is more difficult to affect change, so the young person needs to learn how to tolerate their distress and become more aware of their feelings (rather than fighting them all the time). In addition, we teach the skill of self-acceptance leading to self-soothing. Here, the goal is to increase self-esteem and self-worth.

Session 12: Cribsheet for the therapist

- Acceptance strategies – tolerating the emotion.
- Introduction to mindfulness.
- Self-soothing using all the senses.

Agenda

- Bridge from last session.
- Homework review.
- Any issues raised by the young person (see earlier notes on this).
- Main session topic.
- Homework plan.
- Feedback.

Module 20: Riding the wave

Aim

The overall aim of this module is to teach young people how to keep their feelings under control and tolerate them effectively, rather than allow themselves to be controlled by their feelings.

Main session topic

In order for the young person to achieve control of their feelings, we start by explaining the strategy called 'riding the wave'. Remind the young person that over previous sessions you have looked together at the range of different feelings they experience. Although they might sometimes think that they should not feel certain emotions, in reality feelings can often be helpful. Look back over the 'Feelings are our friends' exercise. Being mindful can mean being aware of and accepting your thoughts and feelings rather than trying to stop them.

Exercise: Riding the wave

Download Worksheet 43: Riding the wave. Tell the young person that they are now about to take a step back from an emotion and observe it. This means that they will simply note the presence of the emotion, but not engage with it or be ruled by it. Explain that the aim is to experience their emotion as a wave that comes and goes. Advise them to stay with it, and remind them, 'You are not ruled by that emotion. You don't necessarily need to act on it. Remember the times when you have felt differently. Remember that the feeling will not remain this intense for ever. It will pass. You just need to ride it out.'

The following tips should help the young person to learn how to 'surf the wave':

- Try not to *block* the emotion.
- Try not to *squash* the emotion and keep it buried.
- Don't try to *get rid* of the emotion.
- Don't *push* it away.
- Don't try to *keep* emotion around.
- Don't *hold on* to it.
- Don't make it any *bigger*.
- Just let it come and go.

Module 21: Being mindful

Aim

The aim of this module is to introduce the young person to mindfulness and the three different states of mind. Note that this is not expected to give the young person a full training in a skill that requires extensive practice. Rather, the goal is to introduce the concept and teach some basic mindfulness taken from Linehan's model used in DBT.(1)

Main session topic

Start by asking the young person if they have ever heard of mindfulness and explore any relevant experiences they have had. Explain that mindfulness is an extremely useful life skill and that you will first discuss its origins and what it is.

Mindfulness originated as an ancient Eastern practice, but this very simple concept has become highly relevant for our lives today. It can be defined as purposefully and non-judgementally paying full attention to the present moment. During our busy lives, our minds wander all the time, we multi-task, or we allow ourselves to dwell on the past or worry about the future. By contrast, when we are mindful, we recognise when our mind starts wandering and we have the ability to bring it back to the present moment. Mindfulness involves *observing* your internal environment without *responding* to it. We all have the tendency to act on our thoughts, and especially our urges; mindfulness helps us to turn the mind's spotlight to where we want it to shine. Explain to the young person that this is a skill that might help them, because, if they feel their mind roaming all over the place, we can practise bringing it back to the here and now (see the exercises at the end of this module).

Mindfulness aims to increase our self-awareness and our awareness of our thoughts and feelings. If the young person can practise regularly, they can achieve the goal of having more options for how to respond in certain situations, rather than always falling back on their 'default', automatic reaction, which can be fuelled by strong emotions.(2)

As we have discussed throughout this book, there are many different ways of seeing the same thing, depending on our state of mind. These states can be divided into three main categories: 'reasonable mind', 'emotional mind' and 'wise mind' (see Worksheet 44: Mindfulness).(3) A person is in a state of 'reasonable mind' when they are able to adopt an intellectual approach. They tend to be quite logical in their thinking and have rational thought processes, focusing on facts. This enables them to problem-solve with little or no emotional experience. By contrast, when a person is in an 'emotional mind' state, their thinking and behaviour are led specifically by whichever emotion(s) they are currently experiencing. Their cognitions are 'hot', which makes it difficult for them to think logically, and facts tend to be distorted along with the emotional state. The 'wise mind' takes the most pertinent parts of the 'emotional mind' and the 'reasonable mind' and then adds intuition or 'gut feeling'.

At this point you should explain to the young person that they will be unable to overcome an 'emotional mind' with a 'reasonable mind'. Similarly, they will be unable to generate feelings with a 'reasonable mind'. Instead, they must go within and integrate the two in order to get into a 'wise mind' state. This might mean not taking things literally: for example, you can feel afraid but that does not necessarily mean that a situation is life-threatening. Another example might be encountered on a shopping trip at the end of a bad day. If you are in an emotional state of mind, you might enter the supermarket, see all the deals they are offering and end up spending more money than you should. And you might spend even more if you are upset and hungry, too. Alternatively, if you are in a reasonable state of mind, you might enter the supermarket with a list of only the food you need and then stick rigidly to that list, even if you see another item that you really want or spot a great deal that you didn't know about earlier. By contrast, if you are in a wise state of mind, you will probably have a short list of essential items, but you will also allow yourself to be a little flexible and buy the item that catches your eye and the great offer.

Being mindful is all about recognising when we are in an emotional or a reasonable state of mind and then balancing this with gut feeling to achieve a wise state of mind. It is fine to have some feelings or strong emotions about certain situations or issues, but not if this completely dominates and dictates our behaviour.

BEING MINDFUL: MARK

Mark is alone in his bedroom. It has been a really bad day and he has just had an argument with his dad. He feels angry and depressed inside. He's listening to depressing hard rock music and he is getting his razor ready to cut his arm.

Exercise: Assessing Mark's state of mind

Ask the young person to look at Mark's situation, then ask them the following three questions:

- Which state of mind do you think Mark is in?

Mark starts to think about the argument with his dad, pieces it together a little, and begins to understand that it developed out of nothing.

- Which state of mind do you think Mark is in now?
- Imagine that Mark is able to go into his wise state of mind. What might happen?

Mark recognises he is feeling angry and depressed and he is able to understand that the argument and the bad day at school led to him feeling this way. He's now in a position to make a decision about what to do next.

Exercise: Exploring the three states of mind

Explain to the young person that the wise state of mind can be seen as:

- Suddenly understanding the meaning or crux of an issue.
- Having clarity of thought or seeing it clearly.
- Being able to see the whole picture rather than the individual parts.
- Getting a sense or 'feeling' that you have come to the right decision. This sense seems to come from deep inside, not from the current emotional state.

Elicit examples of when the young person has acted in each of the three states of mind after illustrating them with the three examples from Jessica.

JESSICA'S EMOTIONAL MIND

Jessica was sick and tired of not being allowed out late on a school night. One day she had an argument with her mum and in the heat of the moment headed off to Brighton even though she had an important exam the next day.

JESSICA'S REASONABLE MIND

Jessica stayed at home and studied for her impending exam.

JESSICA'S WISE MIND

Jessica sat down with her mum and devised a plan: she would study for several hours, then go out with her friends before arriving home at a reasonable hour.

Getting into your wise mind

Download Worksheet 45: How to get into your wise mind.

When you are in your wise mind you are aware of what is happening, how you feel, and what you are thinking and experiencing. In order to get into this state of mind (and enable yourself to make reasonable decisons even when you feel a surge of emotion), you have to appreciate what is going on right at that moment. You almost need to press a 'pause button' and notice – in detail – all that you are experiencing, feeling and thinking. It is like you are stepping into yourself and observing everything that is happening but not trying to change it. It is much easier to enter a wise state of mind when you feel good, and much harder when you feel bad.

Go through the two steps below with the young person, both of which are taken from Linehan's work on mindfulness. Understanding mindfulness in more detail will help the therapist to explain the basic concepts to the young person. Further information is available from Linehan's book and skills manual (see References at the end of this session).

Step 1: Observing

Observing involves sensing or experiencing something without describing or labelling the experience. It is simply turning our attention to something and just noticing it. Ask the young person to turn their attention to what is in their head and what they are experiencing right now. Then ask them to imagine that this moment in time is 'freeze-framed'. It is natural and understandable that we, as human beings, try to stop painful feelings or try to keep hold of the feelings we enjoy. Ask the young person to stay with the awareness, to stay in their wise mind, without trying to change it. The key to this is to recognise when we are judging our thoughts, emotions or sensations as 'good' or 'bad': notice the judgements (but don't enter into them) and try to let them pass. Encourage the young person simply to observe what is happening. They should focus their attention on one thing in the moment and try to let any worries, thoughts and distractions that pop into their head 'float away' (like the judgements), which will allow them to keep returning their focus to the present moment. If this is difficult for them to achieve, suggest spending a few minutes focusing on the sounds they can hear. Do the task with them in silence, then feed back at the end of the time, offering your experiences of this mindfulness task.

Step 2: Describing

This task employs the skill of using words to represent what is observed: no judgements; just a description of 'what is'. Explain this to the young person and ask them to reflect on what is happening right now. Then ask them to describe what is happening in as much detail as they can. Again, you could model this to them with your own examples.

MARK'S DESCRIPTION EXERCISE

Mark was feeling angry after talking to his therapist about the argument he'd had last night with his dad. She asked him to describe what was happening right now, in the session, without interpreting or judging it in any way. He struggled at first, but with the therapist's help he came up with:

continued

> My heart is beating quickly. I am feeling the urge to shout or walk out of here. My back teeth are pressed tightly together, providing a tight sensation in my cheeks. I have the thought in my head 'I hate my dad', which I am trying just to notice, without 'getting into the thought'. I am noticing an urge to 'enter' the thought and now other thoughts are popping into my head about my dad.

Discuss the difference between observing and describing. Observing is sensing without words. Describing a thought requires you to notice that it is a thought, not a fact. There is a significant difference between thinking, 'I'm a failure' and failing. It might be helpful to use the alien analogy. Imagine that an alien has landed from outer space and has no experience of human thoughts or feelings. Your job is to try to explain what is going on in your mind and body.

Mindfulness exercises to practise during this and future sessions

Mindfulness can be a tricky concept to grasp, so it is often useful to try some exercises together. These should enable the young person to get a sense of what the concept is experientially. Two sample exercises are outlined below and there are more on Worksheet 45. It is a good idea to do each exercise with the young person and then share both your own and their experiences of it. If you are not very familiar with mindfulness as a concept, we advise attending a course on the subject, or practising it yourself. Try to fit in a mindfulness exercise during every session from now on, and encourage the young person to practise between sessions, too.

Another good way to illustrate mindfulness could be to look on YouTube for examples and explanations. For example, there is a relatable scene from the film *Kung-Fu Panda*, 'The peach tree of heavenly wisdom'.

Exercise 1

Both the therapist and the young person start to count slowly to ten in their heads. Tell the young person that if they find their mind wandering away from the counting, they should gently bring it back and start again. Do this for up to two minutes, ask for feedback, then give your own experiences of the exercise.

Exercise 2

Introduce a stimulus (such as a pen). Give verbal prompts, such as 'Pay attention to the touch/feel/look/smell of the pen', or verbal instructions as you present the object. Involve all of the senses, but keep the exercise short at first. Normalise the actions of the mind: 'Where did your mind wander off to? How did you find the process? What did you do to get your mind back?' Ask what happened and use the feedback to shape mindfulness as a skill.

How to generate feedback

Remind the young person just to notice urges, judgements, assumptions, comparisons, attachments, memories, interpretations, associations, thoughts, images, sensations, predictions, etc.
Get them to take a meta-cognitive position:

- How did you find the process?
- Where did your mind wander off to?
- What did you do to get it back?
- Although you don't think you are able to do this, notice for a minute that you managed to turn your mind to something of your choosing.
- Avoid inviting interpretations. Don't ask, 'Why . . .?' Use 'What . . .?' questions instead.
- What happened to the urge?
- Is that something that happens outside of the room (e.g. pushing emotions away)?
- Maybe next time you will just notice it and let go?
- Notice when it is effective for you.
- Notice urge–action links and emotional responses. Ask, 'How did the anger manifest itself? Thoughts, feelings, physical sensations, etc. What did you do? What were the consequences?'

See Home-task on Worksheet 45 for practice ideas.

Module 22: Self-soothing

Aim

This is a continuation of the 'acceptance' strategies and the aim is to enable young people to find ways to calm themselves at times of high emotion.

Exercise: Self-soothing

Download Worksheet 46: Self-soothing and together identify some calming strategies that the young person might employ during times of high emotion. It can be useful for the young person to put some of their self-soothing items in a box. Encourage them to engage all of the senses, so, for example: a piece of silk ribbon (for touch), a bar of chocolate (for taste), a favourite perfume (for smell), etc.

End of Session 12

- Homework exercise for Module 20: ask the young person to try 'surfing the emotion' when they experience both a positive emotion and a more negative emotion. They should write down how they got on for discussion in the next session.
- Homework exercise for Module 21: ask the young person to try to get into their wise mind. Without stopping whatever they are doing, they should try to notice how they are doing it and what they are feeling. Worksheet 45 can be used for guidance.
- Homework exercise for Module 22: ask the young person to identify the methods they will try to use over the next week to self-soothe.
- Feedback.

References

1. Linehan, M. (1993) *Cognitive Behaviour Treatment of Borderline Personality Disorder*. New York: Guilford Press; Linehan, M. (1993) *Skills Training Manual for Treating Borderline Personality Disorder (Diagnosis and Treatment of Mental Disorders)*. New York: Guilford Press.
2. Hofmann, S.G., Sawyer, A.T. and Fang, A. (2010) The empirical status of the 'new wave' of cognitive behavioral therapy. *Psychiatric Clinics of North America* 33(3), 701–710.
3. These three categories and the descriptions of mindfulness and mindfulness techniques that follow are adapted from Linehan's two 1993 books, op. cit.

HANDOUT FOR THE YOUNG PERSON: SESSION 12

What are acceptance strategies?

Up to now, this therapy programme has focused on ways to *change* problem behaviours, thoughts and feelings. This session is about *managing* difficult feelings by tolerating them, becoming more aware of them, accepting them and using your own senses to cope with them.

Riding the wave

We've talked about the function of emotions and that although people often think that they *shouldn't* feel certain things, in reality, feelings can often be helpful. Being mindful can mean being aware of and accepting your thoughts and feelings without trying to stop them. All you need to do is to take a step back from the emotion and observe it. This is a bit like being at a busy train station and, instead of getting on the first train that stops and going to a destination you don't know, you stay on the platform and watch the trains (or emotions) come and go. So you simply note the presence of the emotion; you do not engage with it and you are not ruled by it. Just stay with it and ride it like a wave. *You are not your emotion and you don't need to act on it.* Remember times when you have felt different. Remember the feeling will not stay this intense for ever. It *will* pass. You just need to ride it out.
  The following tips should help you surf the wave:

- Try not to *block* the emotion.
- Try not to *squash* the emotion and keep it buried.
- Don't try to *get rid* of the emotion.
- Don't *push* it away.
- Don't try to *keep* emotion around.
- Don't *hold on* to it.
- Don't make it any *bigger*.
- Just let it come and go.

Mindfulness

Gaining mindfulness is very useful, but it takes a bit of time and effort to achieve.

Definition

Mindfulness means purposefully and non-judgementally paying full attention to the present moment. During our busy lives, our minds wander all the time, we multi-task or we allow our minds to dwell on the past or worry about the future. Mindfulness is being able to recognise when our mind wanders and gently bringing it back to the present moment. It is being able to observe our internal environment without responding to it. We all have the tendency to act on our thoughts, especially our urges; mindfulness helps us to turn the spotlight back on to where we want it to go.

In the session, you will have done an exercise or two with your therapist to get an idea of what mindfulness is in practice. Essentially, it can help you to increase your ability to be self-aware and aware of your thoughts and feelings.

As we have discussed before, there are many different ways of seeing the same thing, depending on what frame of mind we are in. One way of looking at these different states of mind is to divide them into three categories:

- Reasonable mind – just focusing on the facts, no emotion.
- Emotional mind – feeling emotional and making decisions and acting on the basis of how you feel.
- Wise mind – the best bits of reasonable and emotional mind, plus your gut instinct.

How to get into your wise mind

When you are in your wise mind you are aware of what is happening, how you feel, and what you are thinking and experiencing. In order to get into your wise mind (and have the ability to make reasonable decisons even when you get a surge of emotion), you have to notice what is going on right in the moment. You almost need to press a 'pause button' and notice in detail all that you are experiencing, feeling and thinking. It is like you are stepping into yourself and observing everything that is going on without trying to change it. It is easier to enter a wise state of mind when you feel good, and much harder when you don't.

Self-soothe

When you feel an intense emotion and become distressed, it may be that self-harm helps to manage or reduce the feeling. Your therapist will have talked to you about organising a self-soothe box. This is a way to bring your emotion down without hurting yourself and using the power of your senses. The box should include nice items for you to see, smell, taste, touch and hear: for example, a favourite music track, a picture of you and your friends having a good time, your favourite perfume, etc.

Session 13

This session comprises one specific module and session focus – alternatives to self-harm (Module 23). Remember there was the option of starting this module at the beginning of therapy, in Session 1. If this option was taken, this is an opportunity to reflect on the alternatives that have been tried and the progress that has been made.

In addition to the focus on alternatives to self-harm, any unfinished issues from previous sessions should be resolved and/or the ongoing strategies the young person is utilising should be explored further.

Session 13: Cribsheet for the therapist

- Alternatives to self-harm.
- What else can you do when you feel overwhelmed and tempted to self-harm?

Module 23: Alternatives to self-harm

Aims

The aim of this module is to enable the young person to consider alternatives to self-harm. Often, they will be so accustomed to utilising self-harm when they are emotionally overwhelmed that they will have no experience or memory of using other, more adaptive, coping strategies. Some will never have learned the skills to manage their intense emotions; others will have forgotten them. This session is an opportunity for them to discover or rediscover those skills.

It should also be used to review ongoing homework tasks, such as thought-challenging, mindfulness techniques, and facing fears; to catch up on any missed or shortened sessions; and to remind the young person of the coping tree and which strategies might be used in which situations.

Agenda

- Bridge from last session.
- Homework review.
- Any issues raised by the young person (see earlier notes on this).
- Main session topic.
- Homework plan.
- Feedback.

Main session topic

After going through the alternative to self-harm that Cassie has found useful, download Worksheet 47: What else can I do? and go through it with the young person.

CASSIE'S ALTERNATIVE TO SELF-HARM

'Sometimes I paint how I feel in my book. The pictures can be pretty gruesome but I don't show anyone – they're just for me.'

Explore whether any of the alternatives on the worksheet have worked for the young person in the past, or if there are any that they would like to try. Ask them to add any extra ones that they have found useful in the past.

It is a good idea to go through a recent example of self-harm (or the one the young person described in Worksheet 3). You could ask them at what point they might have tried one of the alternatives. Also, it is useful to ensure that the alternative strategies are easily accessible to the young person while their preferred method of self-harm is not.

End of Session 13

- Homework: ask the young person to try alternatives to self-harm and monitor how they are getting on.
- Feedback.

HANDOUT FOR THE YOUNG PERSON: SESSION 13

It is not easy to stop self-harming, especially if there is nothing to take its place. This session is about finding alternatives to self-harm.

You may feel you have got into the habit of automatically thinking about self-harm whenever you feel emotionally overwhelmed. Also, you might think that you don't have much experience of using more adaptive coping strategies (or you haven't found one that works for you). It might be that you have never really learned the skills to manage your intense emotions. This is an opportunity for you to discover those skills and strategies.

Your therapist will go over all the homework tasks and strategies that you have found useful so far (for example, thought-challenging, mindfulness techniques, and facing your fears). Try to think back to the coping tree and remind yourself which strategies to use in certain situations. The worksheet is full of examples that other young people have found to be useful alternatives to self-harm. If you are finding it difficult to choose, any activity that changes your temperature (such as a cold shower or an ice bucket), vigorous exercise (such as running on the spot or star-jumps) and muscle relaxation techniques are often good ones to try first.

Part Four

On you go!

The aims of this part are to consolidate all the work you have done in the previous sessions; to focus on relapse prevention; to think about the next steps, post-therapy; to hand over an ending certificate; and to say goodbye.

This is the shortest part of the book. As outlined here, it might comprise four modules delivered in just one session: Module 24: Reviewing goals; Module 25: Identifying triggers; Module 26: First-aid kit and toolbox; and Module 27: My path and certificate. Alternatively, these four modules could be delivered over two (or more) sessions. Some young people find it easy to take on the consolidation and ending exercises, whereas ending therapy and relapse prevention can be a longer process with others. You must be convinced that the young person is leaving treatment with a clear idea of the strategies that they find useful and an understanding of their journey and the development and maintenance of their difficulties (the formulation). It may be that you need to return to specific strategies or concepts and go over them several times.

To reiterate, the number of sessions is not set in stone, so use your clinical judgement and feedback from the young person to decide how many they require during this phase. Only when you are satisfied that they have got everything they can from the programme should you print out their certificate, fill it in, and hand it to them.

Session 14: Cribsheet for the therapist

- Review of goals.
- Relapse prevention – what are my triggers?
- Therapy first-aid kit and toolbox.
- The future.

Session 14

Now is the time to review goals for the last time, administer the end-of-treatment questionnaires and start the relapse prevention – or 'keeping well' – work.

Module 24: Reviewing goals

Aim

The aim of this module is to re-rate the original problems (blind) by reading them out and asking the young person how they rate them now, on a scale of one to ten.

Agenda

- Bridge from last session.
- Homework review.
- Any issues raised by the young person (see earlier notes on this).
- Main session topic.
- Homework plan.
- Feedback.

Main session topic

This is the end of the treatment and an opportunity to re-rate the original problem list and assess how far the young person has progressed. Don't remind them of their first rating until after this exercise because you want a fresh rating.

A lot of young people feel anxious about leaving therapy so it is important for you to empower them to believe in their ability to move on. Now that they have almost completed therapy, the next step is for them to keep working on any problems that arise, using the strategies they have learned over the past few months. Acknowledge their achievements and make a note to put these on the certificate. At this point, it is useful to go over the formulation again and give them a copy to keep.

Module 25: Identifying triggers

Aims

The aims of this module are: to explore possible triggers for new episodes of self-harm; to review the new coping strategies the young person has learned; to assess their ability and readiness to use them, if required; and to help them to think about and identify potential triggers for any self-harm urges in the future.

Exercise: Staying safe

Discuss any potential triggers for self-harm based on your knowledge of the young person and your collaborative formulation. When you have identified these, download Worksheet 48: Staying safe, and list the triggers on the sheet. Use Cassie's example as a guide.

HOW CASSIE PLANS TO STAY SAFE

Cassie was asked to think about the future and write down a list of possible events, people's reactions, feelings and thoughts that could push her into harming herself again.

- Friendship issues, such as feeling let down, arguments, feeling left out.
- Being on my own after a friendship issue and my thoughts going crazy (e.g. catastrophising). I now realise that I can challenge my thoughts when my underlying beliefs are triggered and make myself think in a certain way: for example, 'No one likes me (I'm unlovable).'
- Very strong emotions, in particular when I feel extremely angry mixed with panic (that my worst fears of being not liked will come true).
- My dad saying he'll do something/take me somewhere but then work gets in the way.

Module 26: First-aid kit and toolbox

Aims

The first-aid kit and the toolbox are two exercises for consolidation of acquired skills, relapse prevention and healthy living. The first-aid kit is designed to help the young person review the coping skills they have practised or discussed during therapy and think about what specific skills they might use when they are at a crisis point or struggling after the end of therapy. The toolbox is designed to help the young person keep in mind coping strategies to stabilise internal well-being, stay well and avoid crisis points.

Continuing the journey

In order for the young person to continue on their journey and 'stay well', their life has to have balance. They will need to continue to make and maintain healthy relationships, which will include using their assertiveness skills, anger management skills and other cognitive strategies. Moreover, they will need to identify a network of supportive, trustworthy friends and family (something they should have done on their relationships map, which they could redo now, if they think it would be useful). It is also important for them to identify any people who are more likely to encourage self-destructive patterns of behaviour.

Another important element in keeping well and moving on is to achieve your life goals and maintain your values, as far as possible. These goals and values might be study-related or hobby-related, or they could include other things that help the young person to establish a sense of purpose and meaning in their life.

Overall, young people who have a history of self-harm need to learn to 'take good care of themselves'.(1) This involves maintaining a balance between achievement and fun, accepting support from others and doing things for themselves, and trying to follow a generally healthy lifestyle (through exercise, a good, well-balanced, healthy diet, a regular sleep pattern, etc.). However, it is important to recognise that exceptions to these general rules are acceptable, as long as they do not lead back into self-harm or other dysfunctional behaviours.

The life-plan exercise devised by Lorraine Bell might prove useful at this point.(2)

Exercise: My life plan

Download Worksheet 49: My life plan, and ask the young person to list their personal goals for the next week, month, and so on. They should try to find at least one goal for every area of their life and try to fill in as many of the boxes as possible.

Table 7 My life plan

	Diet	Relationships/ friends	Hobbies	School/ college/ work	Lifestyle	Family
1 week						
1 month						
2–6 months						
6–12 months						
1–2 years						

Exercise: First-aid kit

Download Worksheet 50: First-aid kit and toolbox and explain that this is a 'crisis' first-aid kit: it should be used when the young person is in distress or experiencing intense and difficult emotions. Remind them of the triggers for self-harm they listed in Module 25 and discuss Cassie's first-aid kit.

CASSIE'S FIRST-AID KIT

What Cassie will do to cope when she is in a crisis:

- Have my coping tree readily to hand and remember to stop for a few seconds when I get a surge of emotion and notice what is going through my mind and what I'm feeling. Use looking at the tree to do the self-analysis.
- Be very aware of my thinking and try to let my emotions die down before doing anything. Phone a friend, 'ride the wave', notice my physical sensations and breathe until I calm down.
- If I get a strong urge to self-harm, get out my list of pros and cons of self-harm or think through them again from scratch.
- Read through my therapy worksheets to remind myself that the feeling will pass and I have ways to cope with it.
- Look at my list of thought-challenges and my formulation and remember that I feel this bad only when my beliefs are triggered. It will pass!

Now take the folder of worksheets that the young person has worked through over the past few weeks and your reference book and help them identify which particular strategies they find most useful at specific times and what they would need to get back on track in a time of crisis.

Discuss how ready or able they feel to try out the identified strategies and add the best ones to the spaces in the first-aid kit.

Exercise: Toolbox

It might be useful to work through examples of what the young person feels could be a problem between now and a certain point in the future. Then explore how they would use the toolbox to prevent this; or, if they feel this might be difficult, how they might use the first-aid kit to cope and get back on track. Use Cassie's example as a guide.

CASSIE'S TOOLBOX

What Cassie will do to stay well:

- Make sure I keep up regular scheduling of activities that give me a sense of pleasure and achievement.
- Keep my list of thought-challenges in my phone and the poster I have made on my wall.
- Keep a copy of the coping tree in my phone and on a small laminated card in my purse, so I can easily find the best skill to use when I can't think straight.
- Remember to balance my time, so that I don't end up spending too much time with one friend or just my family. Remember to schedule in 'me time'/'taking care of myself'.
- Continue to practise my assertiveness skills, rather than 'flying off the handle'. The more I practise, the easier it will be to manage my anger.

Module 27: My path and certificate

Aim

The aim of this module is to plan positive aspects for the future and award the programme certificate. This is the end of therapy.

Exercise: My path

Download Worksheet 51: My path, and tell the young person that they are going to look towards the next week, the next month and the next year and think about all the positive things that might happen. They will also schedule regular exciting/interesting events for the immediate future. They should start to write these on the 12-month timeline after looking at Cassie's example.

CASSIE'S PATH

Cassie is looking forward to:

- Next week: Mum cooking spaghetti Bolognese; meeting Sarah in town.
- Next month: finishing my exams; spending more time in the art room; Sarah's birthday party.
- Next few months: going to Lanzarote on holiday; taking my friend's little boy swimming; going to the cinema to see the next big horror film.
- Next year: hosting my own New Year's Eve party; starting dance classes again.

Encourage the young person to think about anything and everything that they might enjoy, including: birthdays, gigs, finishing school, going to a party, watching their favourite TV programme, etc.

The certificate

Download the certificate (see p. 223) and conclude the programme by awarding it to the young person. You should summarise key points you have observed from the sessions spent with the young person in the spaces provided. Think carefully about useful points for feedback that are person-specific, honest and useful for the young person to take away.

KEY POINTS FROM KATY'S CERTIFICATE

- Despite trust issues and tense relationship problems with family, you have taken a risk, trusted me as your therapist and, as a result, you have been able to try out different, more assertive ways of interacting.
- You haven't self-harmed for three months. The scars are fading and you have become very determined with your mindfulness skills and practice. This will be a skill you can use in life and teach your own family. Well done!
- Excellent determination and hard work.

Tell the young person that they have reached the end of the programme successfully. It is a good idea to get some detailed feedback about their views of and reflections on the treatment. This will help them to revise some of the techniques and think about the process and any further help that they feel they might need. It can be useful to suggest to the young person that they schedule individual 'therapy' time every week (generally between ten and thirty minutes, or longer, if feasible). During this time, the young person should look through their folder, think about the week they've had, assess the effectiveness of the strategies they used, and explore others that they might have forgotten.

It is also a useful time to look again at CBT and their formulation and to reflect on any struggles they have had with their emotions, self-harming and relationships. It is all too easy to slip back into unhelpful habits. Explain to the young person that setbacks are likely: most people experience some difficulties after therapy. The key is to deal with them and strengthen the new skills they have learned. Self-harm and other destructive habits can return during times of stress, so the young person must look back over their work and follow the CBT steps whenever they start to feel stressed.

Say goodbye

Remember that the young person has probably put a lot of trust in you as their therapist over the last few months. Ending therapy can be very difficult and the young person may have become strongly attached to you (even if you don't necessarily feel it). Young people can sometimes become so upset towards the end of therapy that they end the sessions early (to avoid feeling rejected) or their symptoms return or increase due to the stress they feel or to keep the therapeutic relationship going. It is important to try to open up the conversation to talk about the issues brought up for the young person by the fact that their therapy is drawing to a close, but you may find it comes up only at the very end. Try to be alert to this throughout the therapy in order to avoid reinforcing any escalation of behaviours.

As was mentioned earlier, it is important to look for such patterns of behaviour early in the process and to address them in good time. A good, well-thought-through formulation and functional analyses of self-harm behaviours should have alerted you to such difficulties, which in turn should enable you to pre-empt any problems that might arise when ending therapy. You will need to think about how you will end the programme. Within the model of CBT, it can be useful practice to offer follow-up sessions, but this might not be appropriate for all young people, particularly those who have developed a very strong attachment and find it difficult to 'let go'. You must be guided by the formulation and clinical need. If the young person is struggling with generalising or implementing the skills, follow-up sessions could be very beneficial. However, if they are more concerned about not seeing the therapist any more, a period of consolidation on their own might be more helpful.

Ending treatment is important for all therapies, whether they are long or short term. The process of therapy helps the young person to be emotionally ready for that therapy to end, and a good therapist will work hard to stop the young person (or their family) becoming dependent on them. One of the key skills when ending is to make sure that the young person's basic emotional needs are being met *outside* of the therapy room. This might be from parents, school or friends, as well as from the skills and strategies the young person has developed during the programme.

Therapists often feel they could offer more at the end of a programme, particularly when problems have not been totally resolved. Remember, though, that the best effects of therapy come from achieving a balance between the therapist's support and the young person's own motivation to implement the strategies they have learned. Hopefully, a parent or carer will be able to take on the supportive role that was played by the therapist during the sessions. It might be worth asking the young person if they are happy for a parent or carer to join the sessions and share their ideas. This can happen from the very beginning if the young person is willing. If not, inviting a parent/carer to the last couple of sessions for feedback can be very useful.

In addition to ensuring that the young person has the necessary tools to continue with their journey, another aspect of saying goodbye is to reflect on the end of therapy. This final session should provide an opportunity for the young person to move on to the next part of their life with new and well-tested strategies to avoid their previous destructive patterns. It is also an opportunity for them to practise tolerating and overcoming the hurt that inevitably accompanies the end of a significant relationship.

End the treatment with general feedback from the young person about the therapeutic journey they have experienced with you. You might ask:

- How have you found this treatment?
- Have there been times when you thought it was particularly useful/ less useful?
- What aspects of the therapy (my therapist style) helped or hindered the process?
- What will you take from this experience?

Try to use the young person's feedback to understand your own style and to add to their formulation and plans for the future. Say goodbye, and give the young person a therapeutic concluding letter with a summary of their treatment, if you feel this would be useful. If not, the certificate and their file of work can mark the transition from their treatment to the next stages of their life.

Reference

1. Bell, L. (2003) *Managing Intense Emotions and Overcoming Self-destructive Habits: A Self-Help Manual.* London: Routledge.
2. Ibid.

HANDOUT FOR THE YOUNG PERSON: SESSION 14

Ending

You have reached the end of your treatment. It is normal to have mixed feelings about this: some people are desperate to finish and get on with their lives; others feel a bit sad and anxious. Both reactions are normal. You have probably put a lot of trust in your therapist over the last few months and made a good connection with them. Try to tell them how you feel; they can support you through the ending process.

Think about the end of your therapy as an opportunity to move on to the next phase of your life, but with some new and well-tested strategies to avoid familiar destructive patterns. It is also an opportunity for you to practise tolerating and overcoming the hurt that always accompanies the end of a significant relationship.

Reviewing goals

You will be going over your goals with your therapist to assess your progress in the areas that you felt were most important for you. Although many people feel much better and self-harm much less after completing the treatment, it is unlikely that you will be left with no problems at all. The trick is to keep trying the strategies and practising the skills, and do your best to use them instead of self-harming. Keep working on any problems that arise. You have done so well to reach the end of the programme and you have made such good progress. Now you need to consolidate it.

Identifying triggers

It is important to prepare yourself for possible triggers for new episodes of self-harm. This will mean you are far less likely to be caught out. Think about what you have learned about your patterns of self-harm and which buttons might be pushed that could tempt you to self-harm again in the future. Also, reflect on the cons of self-harm and the reasons why you wanted to start this treatment in the first place.

First-aid kit and toolbox

The first-aid kit and toolbox pull together all of the most useful skills you have learned during the programme. They should help you to stay well and continue with more healthy living. The first-aid kit includes all of the key skills to use when you reach a crisis point or find yourself struggling. Use it when you are in distress or experiencing intense and difficult emotions. The toolbox will help you to keep in mind all of the coping strategies that might be helpful, or simply to stay well when life gets tough and avoid crisis points.

Healthy living

Remember that you need to continue your journey and stay well. This means that your life has to have balance. You will need to continue to make and maintain healthy relationships, which will include using your assertiveness skills, anger management skills and other cognitive strategies that focus on your thoughts and beliefs. You should already have identified a network of supportive, trustworthy friends and family in your relationships map. (You can redo this now, if you think it would be useful.) You should also list any people who push you towards self-destructive behaviour and avoid them.

Another important aspect to keeping well and moving on is to pursue your own life goals and stick to your values, as far as possible. This could include anything that is important to you personally, such as good grades at school, a hobby, or aspects of a relationship – those things that help you to gain a sense of purpose and meaning in your life.

Overall, you need to learn to take good care of yourself. This involves maintaining a balance between achievement and fun, accepting support from others and doing things for yourself, and trying to follow a generally healthy lifestyle (through exercise, diet, etc.). Don't worry too much about exceptions to this general rule (we all need to have fun and enjoy ourselves sometimes!), as long as these do not lead back into self-harm or other problem behaviours. It might be useful to look through your folder of worksheets from time to time and think about which strategies you have found most useful in particular situations and which you might use to get back on track in times of crisis. Add these to the spaces in the first-aid kit.

My life plan

What are your personal goals for the next week, month, year? Think of goals for all the different areas of your life.

My path

Everybody needs things to look forward to for good mental health and to make positive plans for the future. You should think about all of the positive things that might happen over the next year and schedule regular exciting/interesting events for the immediate future. Try to think about anything and everything that you might enjoy, including: birthdays, gigs, finishing school, going to a party, watching your favourite TV programme, etc.

Finishing therapy

Well done for reaching the end of the programme successfully. To keep up your good progress, you might want to schedule your own individual 'therapy' time every week (ten to thirty minutes; or longer, if you have the time). During these personal sessions, look through your folder, think about the week you've had and the strategies you've used, and which other ones might have been useful. You could also remind yourself about CBT and your formulation, and reflect on any struggles you've had with your emotions, self-harming and relationships.

Don't worry about the odd setback: most people experience some difficulties after therapy. The key is to deal with them and strengthen all of the new skills you have learned. Self-harm and other destructive habits can return during times of stress, so it is extremely important for you to look back over your work and follow the CBT steps whenever you start to feel stressed.

Worksheets

What's going on?

WORKSHEET 1

'Real-life stories'

We talk throughout this programme about 'virtual' stories of four people who have harmed themselves. You may feel you have things in common with some of them. We will introduce them properly later, but for now, here is a snapshot of their stories.

JESSICA

'I've done it for ever . . . I can't imagine what my life would be like if I didn't self-harm'

CASSIE

'The nothingness inside just takes over . . . I cut myself to feel something, anything'

MARK

'I cut myself to get rid of the crap feelings inside . . . I like the sight of my blood, it makes me feel better'

KATY

'The arguments and stress built up inside me until I couldn't handle it anymore . . . that's when I took the pills'

'Time-line of self-harm'

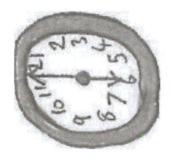

Age

0   18

WORKSHEET 3

'Why you self-harmed'

How you feel before you self-harm

Think of your most recent experience of self-harm and answer any of these you feel comfortable with:

What happened?

What led you to do it?

What did you feel before?

What else was important at the time (events, thoughts, memories, exhaustion, voices, etc.)?

Was there anything else in the background (something current or an echo from the past)?

Did you spend a long time thinking about harming or was it spur of the moment, or both?

Is that your usual way (if not, what was the difference)?

How you feel after you self-harm

Think of your most recent experience of self-harm and answer any of these you feel comfortable with.

How did you feel immediately afterwards?

How did you feel a bit later?

How do you feel about it now?

How do you think your self-harm has helped?

How do you think it doesn't help?

Is there anything you would have done differently?

Is that your usual way (if not, what was the difference)?

How do you feel now?

WORKSHEET 4

'Problems and goals'

Problems and goal setting

Problems (score 0–10)	Goals

'What is CBT?'

The Cognitive-Behavioural model – what's it all about?

Cognitive Behaviour Therapy is an effective way of helping people to deal with their problems. It explores the link between what we think, how we feel and what we do, our behaviour.

For example:

Thinking that you are not very good at talking with people may make you **feel** very worried when you are out with your friends. You may **go quiet (behaviour)** and not talk very much.

Thinking that no one likes you may make you **feel** sad. You may **stay at home** on your own.

Thinking that you never get things right may make you **feel** angry. You may **cut yourself** to get rid of this feeling. You may then **feel** sad because, yet again, you have **done something wrong**.

> Let's look at a more detailed example and think about how the thoughts that go through your mind affect how you feel and what you do (your behaviour).

WORKSHEET 6

'Help triangle'

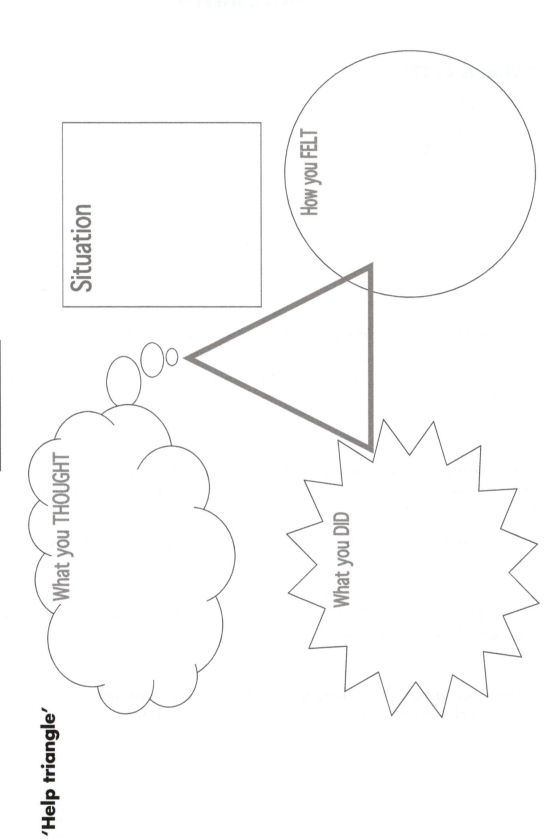

Situation

What you THOUGHT

How you FELT

What you DID

WORKSHEET 7

'Unmixing the feeling cocktail'

Session tasks:

We are going to look at your feelings in more detail. Look at this list of different feelings and, following my instructions, point to three different feelings, one at a time.

When you pick one, read it out loud and tell me what you think it means in your own words. (It's not a test and some are difficult, but just let me know how you understand it.)

- Can you give me an example of when you have recently felt like this or when a friend/relation has felt like this?
- Can you try to describe exactly what was happening when you felt like this?
- Now can you do the same for the other feelings you have picked and describe how another young person your age might behave and what they might be thinking if they felt like this?

WORKSHEET 8

'Emotions list'

Emotions

Scared	Afraid	Confident	Brave	Happy	Content
Lonely	Tearful	Calm	Hurt	Anxious	Disgusted
Disgusting	Out of control	Relaxed	Jealous	Proud	Ashamed
Embarrassed	Frustrated	Miserable	Disappointed	Helpless	Exploited
Furious	Uncomfortable	Love	Sad	Guilty	Excited
Worried	Bored	Annoyed	Used	Grumpy	Mad
Upset					

WORSHEET 9

'Feelings scale'

10
9
8
7
6
5
4
3
2
1
0

WORKSHEET 10

'Emotions diary'

Keeping an emotion diary

Keeping a diary of your feelings can be helpful in a number of ways. By looking back at the diary, you might discover that there is a link between what you were doing and how you felt. You might find that your feelings are stronger at certain times of day, or that they are not as frequent as you thought they were.

How to fill in the diary sheet

The diary sheet breaks down each day of the week into one-hour boxes. In each box, write down the following information:

- What you were doing and who you were with
- How you felt and the strength of the feeling on a scale of 0 to 10 (where 10 is the strongest)

You do not need to write in any detail, just a word or two will do.

8–9 am						
9–10 am			Morning			
10–11 am						
11–12 pm						
12–1 pm						
1–2 pm			Afternoon			

2–3 pm						
3–4 pm						
4–5 pm						
5–6 pm						
6–7 pm						
7–8 pm						
8–9 pm						
9–10 pm						
10–11 pm						
11–12 am						

Afternoon

Evening

WORKSHEET 11

'Feelings are our friends'

Okay, so maybe that sounds a bit silly, but it's true! Think about it for a minute . . .

Most people would say that happiness is a positive feeling, and that anger is a negative feeling, almost one that you shouldn't have at all. But we all have lots of different feelings at different times, even if some of them are pretty unpleasant! It's not bad to feel angry; it's what you do with the feeling that counts.

Let us consider some of the positive aspects of some of the more 'difficult' feelings . . .

ANGER: Can give you strength to stand up for something
What does my anger do for me?

....

ENVY: Can help you strive for something
When has being envious helped me?

....

GUILT: Can help you change how you act
How has feeling guilty helped me?

....

FEAR: Can help you to protect yourself
How has my fear helped me?

....

SHAME: Can help you to be more considerate of those you love in the future
How has it helped me to feel shame?

....

SADNESS: Can help you to move on
How has my sadness helped me?

....

DISAPPOINTMENT: Can help you to be more realistic in your expectations of others and yourself
When has my disappointment helped me?

....

What have you found out about yourself from doing this exercise?

....

....

....

'What feelings do I squash, bottle or swallow?'

SQUASHED FEELINGS

Self-harm is often considered to be a way of managing overwhelming feelings such as anger, frustration, despair or sadness.

Sometimes it can feel like these intense feelings are so great that they will overflow like a volcano and this might be too much to handle. So, when we experience these feelings, we often try to find a way to manage them. Sometimes we might swallow our feelings or bottle them up in order to feel in control of them and some people may harm themselves to get relief.

For some young people, it can be difficult even to know how to describe such intense feelings. By unmixing the feelings cocktail earlier on, you may feel more able to identify and understand your feelings. The next task is to help you to identify those particular feelings that you try to squash or bottle up . . .

'What feelings do I bottle up?'

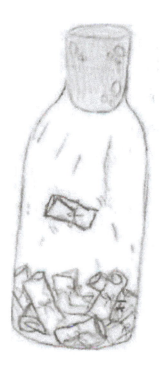

'What feelings do I swallow?'

WORSHEET 13

'My relationship map'

Place yourself at the centre of the following diagram and then add the other people in your life.

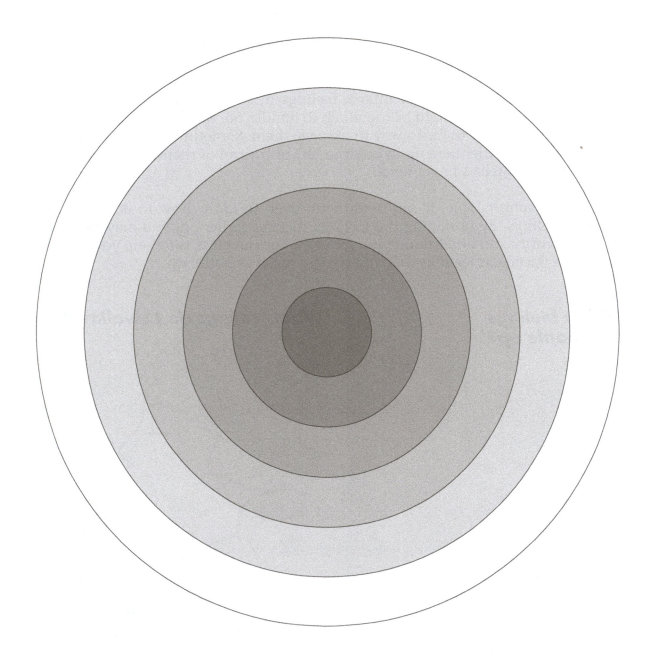

WORKSHEET 14

'Strengths'

My strengths – things I'm good at!

What I'm good at.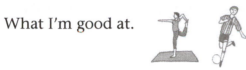

What would your family say are your strengths?

Why my friends like me.

Things I've achieved.

WORKSHEET 15

'Are you ready to make changes?'

The fact that you are reading this means that at least a small part of you is considering change. Any decision about change is not easy as it involves juggling mixed feelings. The following rulers may be able to help you.

Importance of change:
Ask yourself the following questions. How important is it for you to change? What are your reasons and needs for change? What score would you give yourself out 10?

0	1	2	3	4	5	6	7	8	9	10

Ability to change:
Ask yourself the following questions. How confident are you in your ability to change? What score would you give yourself out of 10?

0	1	2	3	4	5	6	7	8	9	10

Once you have rated yourself on both rulers think about the following questions?

- Why have you given yourself this score rather than a 0 or 10?
- What needs to happen to give you a higher score?
- What would you notice about yourself if you had a higher score?
- How would other people be able to help you to get a higher score?
- What strengths and supports do you have that would help you to get a higher score?

How much do other people close to you want you to change?
Mark this on the line below

0	1	2	3	4	5	6	7	8	9	10

If there is a big difference between your own rating and that of other people, what does that tell you?

Reflection box: What have I learned from this?

'Getting things into balance'

It is very easy to feel pressurised by people around you to give up your self-harm. It is likely that your self-harm means a lot of different things to you, some positive and some negative, and that at different times you feel differently about it. So let us try to step back and look at the good and not so good aspects of harming yourself in your life, now and in the future.

Complete the balance sheets below:

Good things about my self-harm for me <u>now</u> . . .	Not so good things about my self-harm for me <u>now</u> . . .
Good things about my self-harm in relation to other people <u>now</u> . . .	Not so good things about my self-harm in relation to other people <u>now</u> . . .
Good things about my self-harm for me <u>in the future</u> . . .	Not so good things about my self-harm for me <u>in the future</u> . . .
Good things about my self-harm in relation to other people <u>in the future</u> . . .	Not so good things about my self-harm in relation to other people <u>in the future</u> . . .

WORKSHEET 17

'Looking at self-harm through other peoples' eyes'

(Role-play)

The aim of this task is for you to look at your self-harm through the eyes of other people. With your therapist, you are going to act out the following situations. Your therapist will pretend to be you each time and you will imagine you are . . .

1. An adult figure like a teacher, family friend, favourite aunt or parent. It should be someone you know will be fair and whom you respect. If you do not know someone like that, make him or her up. It could be someone from TV, a film, a book, or a character from history who has these qualities.

In a letter write what you think this person would say to you about how they understand and see your self-harm. Explain the advice you think they would give you on how to change your life for the better (5 minutes).

2. A close and kind friend. Imagine someone whom you deeply trust who will accept you, no matter what. Again if you can't think of anyone like that in your life, invent such a friend.

How does your friend see you? How has your self-harm affected them?

What are their thoughts and feelings? What advice do they have for you and your future?

Again, talk to your therapist as you imagine your friend would talk to you (5 minutes).

3. Yourself (when you are older and wiser) talking to yourself (now) about your self-harm.

What would you tell yourself? Talk to your therapist in the way you would like the 'future you' to talk to you as you are now (5 minutes).

Reflection box: Spend the final 5 minutes thinking back over what you have talked about. Briefly write down what you've learned from this . . .

Looking at self-harm through other people's eyes

(Letter writing)

The aim of this task is for you to look at your self-harm through the eyes of other people. Take a piece of paper and write three letters to yourself, one from each of the following three people (spend 5 minutes on each letter) . . .

 1. An adult figure like a teacher, family friend, favourite aunt or parent. It should be someone you know will be fair and whom you respect. If you do not know someone like that, make him or her up. It could be someone from TV, a film, a book, or a character from history who has these qualities.

In the letter write what you think this person would say to you about how they understand and see your self-harm. Explain the advice you think they would give you on how to change your life for the better.

 2. A close and kind friend. Imagine someone whom you deeply trust, someone who will accept you, no matter what. Again, if you can't think of anyone like that in your life, invent such a friend.

Imagine you are your friend writing to explain things to you from their point of view.

How does your friend see you? How has your self-harm affected them?

What are their thoughts and feelings? What advice do they give for you and your future?

3. Yourself (when you are older and wiser) writing to yourself (now) about your self-harm.

What would you tell yourself?

Reflection box: Spend a final 5 minutes looking back over what you have written. Briefly write down what you've learned from this . . .

WORKSHEET 18

'Thinking about the future'

Another task that can help you think about whether you're ready to change is to think about how things might be in the future if . . .

1 = you still self-harm
2 = you no longer self-harm

1. Still self-harm	A few years into the future if I still self-harm, the following will have happened in these areas . . .
How fit I am	
How much I enjoy life	
How easy I will find it to get a job	
How easy it will be to finish education	
How happy I feel about my body	
How good I feel about myself	
How much exercise I get	
Having friendships	
Having a boyfriend/girlfriend	
Having a close relationship with my parents	
Having a close friend	
Going on holidays	
Having hobbies/interests	

2. No longer self-harm	A few years into the future, after I have stopped harming myself, the following will have happened in these areas . . .
How fit I am	
How much I enjoy life	
How easy I will find it to get a job	
How easy it will be to finish education	
How happy I feel about my body	
How good I feel about myself	
How much exercise I get	
Having friendships	
Having a boyfriend/girlfriend	
Having a close relationship with my parents	
Having a close friend	
Going on holidays	
Having hobbies/interests	

Reflection box: What have I learned from these two exercises?

FORWARD THINKING EXERCISE

One evening in the next week, spend some time doing this exercise.

Close your eyes and imagine yourself in the future

If you are 16 or 17, imagine that you have just had your 18th birthday.
If you are younger than 16, imagine that you have just had your 16th birthday.

Then open your eyes and write yourself two letters

In the first letter, describe what your life looks like if you have stopped self-harming.
In the second letter, describe what your life looks like if you are still self-harming.

Feeling, thoughts and behaviour

WORKSHEET 19

'Positive pleasant events'

1. Soaking in the bath	41. Flying a kite
2. Planning activities for the future	42. Playing a game
3. Relaxing	43. Singing around the house
4. Taking some 'me' time	44. Arranging flowers
5. Listening to music	45. Going to the beach
6. Going to watch a film	46. Thinking that I'm an OK person
7. Going for a walk	47. Meeting up with an old friend
8. Lying in the sun	48. Going skating
9. Recalling funny/happy memories	49. Reading jokes from a joke book
10. Laughing	50. Sleeping
11. Listening to others	51. Playing a musical instrument
12. Reading a magazine/book	52. Writing poems/stories
13. Talking to people	53. Going to a beauty parlour
14. Picturing a beautiful place	54. Photography
15. Going shopping	55. Daydreaming
16. Thinking about going shopping (!)	56. Watching my favourite programme
17. Doodling	57. Going for a bike ride
18. Looking after a plant or pet	58. Buying gifts
19. Meeting new people	59. Completing a task
20. Planning what I might do if I won the lottery	60. Planning what a date would be like with someone I am attracted to
21. Painting my nails	61. Thinking about pleasant events
22. Writing in my diary	62. Doing something creative
23. Doing a puzzle	63. Dancing
24. Going on a picnic	64. Taking the first step towards a goal
25. Reflecting on the day-to-day things I have achieved	65. Thinking 'I did pretty well' after doing something
26. Buying myself occasional treats	66. Meditating
27. Talking on the phone	67. Playing cards
28. Going to a museum	68. Having an interesting discussion
29. Getting a massage	69. Positive self-talk
30. Reminding myself of my good qualities	70. Doing some voluntary work in the community
31. Surprising someone with a random act of kindness	71. Planning where my favourite place in the world would be to visit
32. Going bowling	72. Going somewhere different for a day
33. Doing a good deed for the day	73. Playing a computer game
34. Sitting in a café and people-watching	74. Going to an aquarium
35. Writing someone a letter	75. Looking at a nice view
36. Doing something new	76.
37. Going horse-riding	77.
38. Making something	78.
39. Having a sauna or jacuzzi	79.
40. Doing a jigsaw puzzle	80.

WORKSHEET 20

'Cassie's activity schedule'

DAY → TIME ↓	MONDAY
8–9 am	Lying awake in bed SAD 9
9–10 am	Got up late for school SAD 7
10–11 am	In English lesson WORRIED 4
11–12 pm	Still in lesson WORRIED 5
12–1 pm	Lunch break alone SAD 10
1–2 pm	In PE with friends WORRIED 8
2–3 pm	In English OK 5
3–4 pm	Walk home from school OK 6
4–5 pm	Tea with mum IRRITATED 7
5–6 pm	Up in my room MISERABLE 8
6–7 pm	Talked to my sister HAPPY 6
7–8 pm	Dinner with family BORING 7
8–9 pm	Watch TV RELAXED 8
9–10 pm	
10–11 pm	Went to bed WORRY 8
11–12 am	Can't sleep WORRY 10

WORKSHEET 21

'Blank activity schedule'

DAY → TIME ↓	Monday	Tuesday	Wednesday	Thursday	Friday	Saturday	Sunday
8–9 am							
9–10 am							
10–11 am							
11–12 pm							
12–1 pm							
1–2 pm							
2–3 pm							
3–4 pm							
4–5 pm							
5–6 pm							
6–7 pm							
7–8 pm							
8–9 pm							
9–10 pm							
10–11 pm							
11–12 am							

'Mark's help triangle'

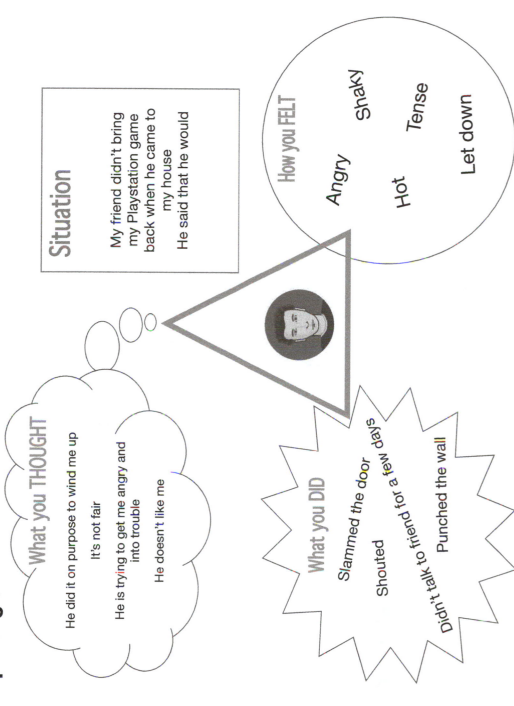

Situation

My friend didn't bring
my Playstation game
back when he came to
my house
He said that he would

How you FELT

Angry   Shaky

Hot   Tense

Let down

What you THOUGHT

He did it on purpose to wind me up

It's not fair

He is trying to get me angry and
into trouble

He doesn't like me

What you DID

Slammed the door

Shouted

Didn't talk to friend for a few days

Punched the wall

'Blank help triangle'

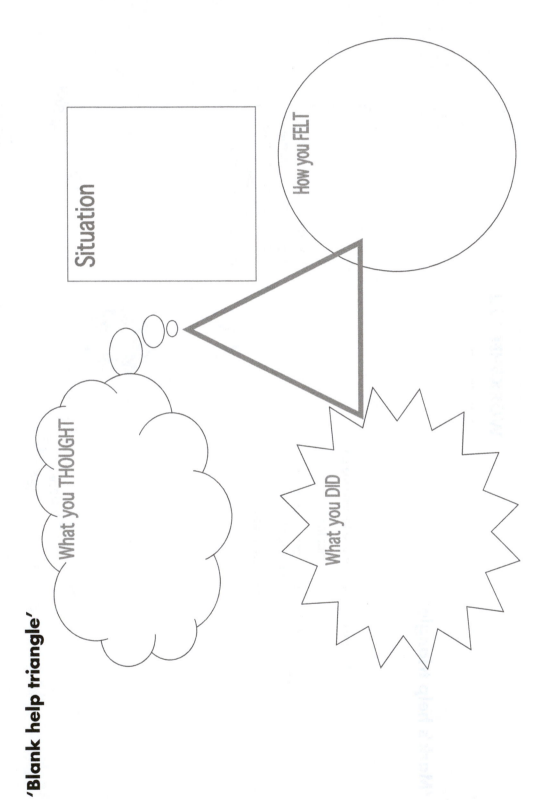

Situation

What you THOUGHT

How you FELT

What you DID

'Glasses'

Jumping to conclusions

1 + 2 = 5 ?

Black-and-white glasses

Over-generalising
Blowing things out
of proportion

Blame yourself glasses

'I should/must/ought' glasses

WORKSHEET 25

'Thinking pitfalls'

You may have heard the expression *'looking through rose-tinted spectacles'* to describe someone who always sees things in a hopeful or cheerful way even when things are bad. This is a kind of thinking pitfall because it is unrealistic.

The person <u>sees the situation from only one viewpoint</u> and does not see the negative aspects of the situation.

Thinking pitfalls or biases are unhelpful ways of thinking. Everyone makes these pitfalls, but when they happen regularly, they can make you feel bad and affect your behaviour.

There are many different types of thinking pitfalls, but the are five main ones to look out for are:

1. Black-and-white thinking

Looking at things in an 'all-or-nothing' way. For example, someone who sees things as being either wonderful or terrible, total success or complete failure, etc., with nothing in between.

2. Jumping to conclusions

Thinking that you know how someone else thinks or feels ('mind-reading') or thinking that you know what will happen ('fortune-telling'). For example, not sitting a test because you 'know' you will fail or thinking that someone no longer likes you because they did not say hello.

3. Over-generalising

Blowing things out of proportion, you can often spot these when there is an 'always', 'never', 'everyone' or 'no one' in the thought. For example, getting a bad grade and thinking, '*Everyone* else is better than me, I am *never* any good at *anything*.'

4. Should/must/ought

Giving yourself a hard time! 'I must do better', 'I should be better', 'I ought to have known better'. These are often linked with over-generalisations 'I should always . . .', etc.

5. Blaming yourself

When you feel responsible for things that are not your fault or that are beyond your control: 'My dad left because of my behaviour', 'It is my fault that I got beaten up', etc.

Don't worry if all of the above sound familiar to you! They are all pitfalls that everyone makes. You may find that you do one more than the others or that you combine different types of thinking pitfalls.

WORKSHEET 26

'The thought record'

Situation	What were you feeling? Scale rating	What thoughts were going through your mind? (NATs)	How much do you believe thoughts? %	What evidence supports your belief in these thoughts?	What evidence challenges your belief?	Can you spot thinking pitfalls?	How much do you believe thoughts now? %	Possible alternative thoughts	How do you rate feelings now?

WORSHEET 27

'The belief scale'

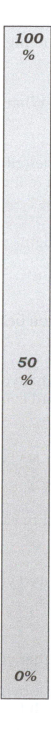

100
%

50
%

0%

WORKSHEET 28

'Quick reference guide'

Ask the young person to record the following when they next experience an unpleasant mood or troubling thought:

1. The Situation

    • Where were you? What were you doing? When? With whom?

2. Feelings

    • Use one word to describe each of your feelings at the time.
    • Rate their strength (out of 100%).

3. Thoughts

    • Describe any thoughts you noticed going through your mind.
    • NATs?

4. Beliefs

    • Rate how much you believe each thought (%).

5. Balancing

    • Record evidence that you can see supports your thoughts.
    • Look for and record evidence that challenges your thoughts.

6. Thinking Pitfalls

    • Look back at your NATs. Can you spot any thinking pitfalls?

7. Beliefs Again

    • Re-rate your belief in each thought (%). Has it changed?

8. Alternative Thoughts

    • Now you've balanced your thought out, try to think of more weighed-up or balanced thoughts.

9. Feelings Again

    • Think about whether your feelings have changed and record this.

TIPS! It can sometimes be helpful to imagine someone (such as a best friend, sister, brother, etc.) and think, 'If they had the same problem/thought, what would I say to them about how they were thinking?'

After using the chart a few times have you noticed that you tend to make the same types of thinking pitfalls over and over again?

WORKSHEET 29

'Sample thought record – Katy's situation'

Situation	What were you feeling? Scale rating	What thoughts were going through your mind? (NATs)	How much do you believe thoughts? %	What evidence supports your belief in these thoughts?	What evidence challenges your belief?	Can you spot thinking pitfalls?	How much do you believe thoughts now? %	Possible alternative thoughts	How do you rate feelings now?
Argument with my best friend	Angry (100%) Hurt (90%) Cheated (75%)	I'm unvalued. I have never meant anything to her. I'm pathetic.	100% 80% 60%	She often makes me feel worthless. She seems to pick fights to upset me and break our friendship.	We are both strong personalities with different ideas. Afterwards, we can laugh about the disagreement.	Over-generalising	60%	It's OK to disagree. I can still be important to someone even (especially?) if we argue.	Angry (40%) Hurt (60%) Cheated (30%)

WORKSHEET 30

'Help with challenging yourself'

Challenge yourself!!

We have seen that, at times, we can all fall into 'thinking pitfalls'. Thinking in these ways can make us experience some unpleasant feelings, like sadness, anger, etc.

 Sometimes we are self-critical and we start to accept these thoughts as true facts. Checking these thoughts out, and challenging them, can help to stop them going round and round in our heads. If we don't challenge them, we can end up feeling worse. Remember the help triangle?! (What we think affects how we feel and what we do.)

Challenging your thoughts is not just about thinking positively about things; it is about having *balanced thinking*. Balanced thinking involves looking for evidence to *support & challenge your thought/problem*.

How to challenge yourself . . . using a thought record

When you next experience an unpleasant mood or troubling thought use the chart and record the following:

1. Record the situation

   • Where were you? What were you doing? When? With whom?

2. Feelings

   • Use one word to describe each of your feelings at the time.
   • Rate their strength using your feelings scale (out of 10).

3. Thoughts

   • Describe any thoughts you noticed going through your mind.
   • NATs?

4. Beliefs

   • Rate how much you believe each thought (%).
   • Use the belief scale.

5. Balancing

- Record evidence that you can see supports your thoughts.
- Look for and record evidence that challenges your thoughts.

This is hard, but your therapist will practise with you.

6. Thinking pitfalls

- Look back at your NATs. Can you spot any thinking pitfalls?

7. Beliefs again

- Re-rate your belief of each thought (%). Has it changed?

8. Alternative thoughts

- Now that you've balanced your thought, try to think of more weighed-up or balanced thoughts.

9. Feelings again

- Think about whether your feelings have changed and record this.

TIPS!

It can sometimes be helpful to imagine someone (such as a best friend, sister, brother, etc.), and think, 'If they had the same problem/thought, what would I say to them about how they were thinking?'

WORKSHEET 31

'The pen-friend, or new Facebook friend'

Imagine you are writing to a pen-friend, someone who has never met you, and you are describing yourself.

Use the following prompts to fill in the details (can be discussed with your therapist).

I am ....

Other people see me as ......

Other people are ....

Relationships are ....

The world is ....

The future is ....

My main CORE BELIEFS are:

My CORE BELIEFS lead to these RULES OF LIVING:

WORKSHEET 32

'Jessica's formulation'

Why me?

Early experiences: Sister was the 'golden child', I was bullied at school, mum was depressed, at home there was a lack of expression of emotion and no arguments

My beliefs and rules of living (based on pen-friend exercise and early experiences)

I'm not good enough/I'm unlovable

Other people's needs always come first

If people disagree with me, **then** they don't like me OR
Other people's opinions are more important than mine

Why now?

What happened before (my problems got really bad)?

Broke up with my boyfriend

Why still?

What keeps my problems going?

Avoiding going out, not getting close to anyone, not telling people how I'm feeling

Good stuff!

What helps?

Listening to music, cousin phoning, forcing myself to go to friend's (small) party, my positive self-statements and challenges to my crucial thoughts

WORKSHEET 33

'My journey' (formulation)

Why me?

> Early experiences

> My beliefs and rules of living (based on pen-friend exercise and early experiences)

Why now?

> What happened before (my problems got really bad)?

Why still?

> What keeps my problems going?

Good stuff!

> What helps?

'Mark's core belief'

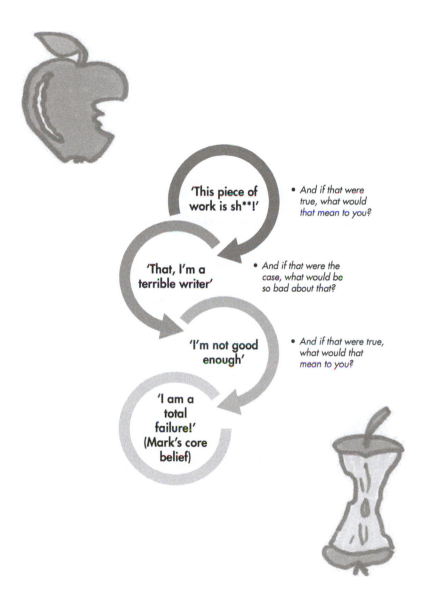

'This piece of work is sh**!'

- *And if that were true, what would that mean to you?*

'That, I'm a terrible writer'

- *And if that were the case, what would be so bad about that?*

'I'm not good enough'

- *And if that were true, what would that mean to you?*

'I am a total failure!' (Mark's core belief)

WORKSHEET 35

'Cassie's core belief'

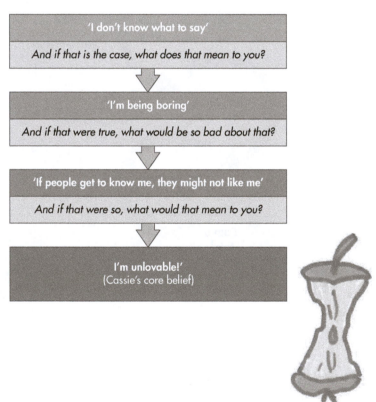

'I don't know what to say'

And if that is the case, what does that mean to you?

'I'm being boring'

And if that were true, what would be so bad about that?

'If people get to know me, they might not like me'

And if that were so, what would that mean to you?

I'm unlovable!'
(Cassie's core belief)

Coping strategies

WORKSHEET 36

'The coping tree'

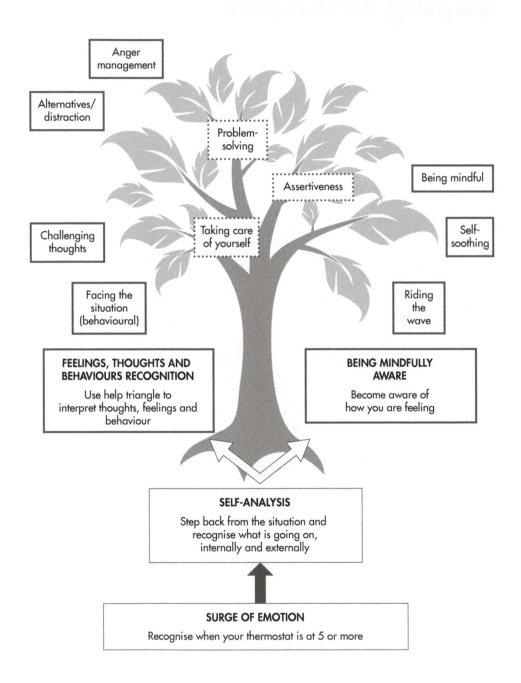

Anger management

Alternatives/distraction

Problem-solving

Assertiveness

Being mindful

Challenging thoughts

Taking care of yourself

Self-soothing

Facing the situation (behavioural)

Riding the wave

FEELINGS, THOUGHTS AND BEHAVIOURS RECOGNITION

Use help triangle to interpret thoughts, feelings and behaviour

BEING MINDFULLY AWARE

Become aware of how you are feeling

SELF-ANALYSIS

Step back from the situation and recognise what is going on, internally and externally

SURGE OF EMOTION

Recognise when your thermostat is at 5 or more

WORKSHEEET 37

'Problem-solving'

Hassles and problems are part of everyday life. Parents, friends, boy- or girlfriends, school, work – in fact almost everything – can create problems in your life at some time or another. Luckily, we are usually quite good at coping with many of our problems and are able to sort them out quickly and successfully.

Other problems seem more difficult. This may be because:

- They happen fairly often
- They have been around for some time
- They feel totally overwhelming – this can happen with either one big problem or lots of smaller problems
- They seem to affect everything you do.

Sometimes these problems take over and life becomes one big worry. Other times, when you try to solve it this makes things worse, or doesn't have the effect you want, or all the solutions you can think of have a downside; so you feel caught between the devil and the deep blue sea. Problem-solving can be as simple as making a decision about what to have for breakfast, or can be more complicated, such as deciding which A-levels to choose, or how to make up with a good friend. It is important to tackle problems rather than avoid them (even if we don't feel like thinking about them). Otherwise we can become overwhelmed by feelings or by the attempt to find the 'perfect' solution.

Learning how to sort out problems and finding ways to try to solve them (or at least have a go!) is what we'll do in this module.

Katy

'I don't know what to do. It's awful! It happened yesterday! What happened was I was on the bus with my so-called mate Shelley and we were talking about my other mate Lennie. I only said he was nice! But she got totally the wrong end of the stick and I arrived at school this morning and everyone's talking behind my back! Lennie's girlfriend is giving me evil looks and I'm scared she's gonna hit me. Everyone's laughing at me! I can't ever go back to school!'

Jessica

'This always happens! I'm sick of his stupid rules, he makes my mum do what he thinks and he doesn't even live at home! Why can't he just leave me alone and let me have a life?! This time it is about this gig that everyone is going to! It's so stupid. I'm not allowed to go because apparently it finishes "too late for a school night". Who does he think he is? He has never cared about me before!'

Step 1: Identify, what is the problem?

> • How is Kate going to deal with her friend, Lennie and the other people at school?

Step 2: List every possible solution

1. Never go to school again
2. Send Shelley a nasty email
3. Arrange a fight with Lennie's girlfriend
4. Kiss Lennie
5. Ignore people laughing
6. Go home, cry and take some tablets
7. Confront Shelley and try to sort it out
8. Talk to Lennie and his girlfriend about what really happened
9. Ask another friend to talk to Lennie
10. Tell a teacher

Step 3: Assess each possible solution

Possibility	Pros	Cons
1	• I don't need to feel embarrassed • I don't like school anyway	• My dad would kill me • I won't get any GCSEs or get into college • They'll think they've won and I'm weak • I'll lose all my friends

Etc . . .

Step 4: Choose the best solution or combination of solutions (this might be the one that has more pros than cons, or the one that you are happy to have a go at).

> 8: Talk to Lennie and his girlfriend because, although it won't be easy, there are more pros than cons for this.
>
> 5: Ignore the laughing because I don't want them to feel they've won!

Step 5: Plan how to carry out the best solution

> - Jot down what I want to say so it's clear in my head
> - Plan a good time to catch Lennie with his girlfriend on their own (after English)
> - Let them know that I want to *talk* to them, not fight
> - Explain the situation that I only like him as a friend and I'm not trying to steal him from her! Shelley got it all wrong.
> - Make sure I've got my friend to talk to afterwards.

Step 6: Review how it's going

- What obstacles might get in the way?
- How might you deal with them?
- What is your plan B?

This could work and your problem will be solved, which is great!!!
But if it doesn't, remember you've got lots of other options to try, like in Katy's case . . .

> I tried really hard to find them on their own but there were always loads of people with them. I just couldn't do it in front of everyone else!!
> So I wrote them a note and it's all okay again now.

Problem-solving

Step 1: Identify, what is the problem?

Step 2: List every possible solution

Step 3: Assess each possible solution

Possibility	Pros	Cons

Step 4: Choose the best solution or combination of solutions

Step 5: Plan how to carry out the best solution. Think about what support you might need to carry this out

Step 6 Review how it's going

- What obstacles might get in the way of your plan?
- How might you deal with them?
- What is your plan B?

WORKSHEET 38

'Assertiveness'

Saying what you really feel and negotiating what you want

Do you sometimes find yourself going along with something when you don't really want to, and then feeling angry or upset with people afterwards?

It is not always easy to say 'no' to someone, especially a friend, and this can be particularly hard when you want to fit in and don't want to be different. You might worry that if you say what you really feel, then people won't like you. The idea of not being liked is pretty horrible, so you could end up under pressure to do things you don't really want to do, like: telling people your private details, taking drugs, skipping school or going to a party or club that you don't want to be at.

When you think about it, though, always going along with others and trying to please them usually ends up with you feeling worse and other people actually respecting you less.

Standing up for your rights can mean saying 'no' or giving your opinion when it is different to others. There are different ways you can do this.

For example, it can be done in an aggressive way with shouting or threatening; this way usually does not work very well because it just makes the other person angry and leads to an argument. Alternatively, it can be done in an assertive way, which means you stand up for yourself, but try to be mindful of the other person's feelings and wishes too. This way can work very well, but a lot of young people find it really hard to do (and so do many adults!).

Look at Cassie's example:

> 'Although it was a huge effort, I did go to my friend's party but when we left, my friends decided to go on to another house party. I didn't want to because I felt too drunk and miserable, and I just wanted to go home.'

'Pleasing others' response	Aggressive response	Assertive response
'I ended up going and hated it! And then I got into a lot of trouble as I had to get my step-dad to pick me up. I felt so crap I went home and cut my arm really badly. I wish I'd stuck to what I wanted to do.'	'None of them appreciated I'd come out when I didn't want to and said I was selfish if I wanted to go home. I went mad and told them all to f*** off. When they left I threw my bottle after them. The neighbour called the police and I've lost *all* my friends!'	'I really didn't want to go and so I said I was really tired and that I'd had enough. They were disappointed and tried to persuade me but I didn't budge. Eventually my friend Sally said she was tired too and she'd come with me. We had a really good chat on the way home.'

Have you got any examples of when you were not as assertive as you would have liked? Maybe you were a 'people pleaser' or got aggressive?

What happened afterwards? How did you feel? What did you do?

What would you have liked to have done or said?

Think of someone you respect/admire for being able to stand up for themselves (e.g., friend, family member, celebrity or character on TV).
How would they respond?

How do you become assertive?

Preparation

What I want to say

Describe the situation or problem that is important to you rather than focusing on the other person or their actions. Try to be as specific as you can. E.g.:

> 'I can see you all want to go to the other party.'

My feelings

Say how you feel about the situation or problem. E.g.:

> 'I am sorry/sad I won't be able to go with you to the party.'

My needs

Say what you want to happen that respects your own needs. E.g.:

> 'I need to go home to go to bed.'

The outcome

The way that you assert yourself and behave will improve the situation for you and the other person. E.g.:

> 'If you all go to the party and I go home, we will all be happier.'

Some strategies to try!!

When you want to stick to your guns, try imagining you are an old style vinyl record that has got stuck, or a CD that is scratched saying 'no' or expressing your opinion over and over again. In spite of what the other person says or does just keep repeating the same thing.

Write out what you want to say before hand and 'rehearse'.

If you are feeling pressurised in any way try ignoring what the other person is saying or doing. This can be really hard to do, but it sends a powerful message!

'SCRIPT IT'

'IGNORE'

'BROKEN RECORD'

'TURN THE TABLES'

'ACT COOL'

'GIVE TO GET'

Concentrate on acting confident, even if you don't feel it! Imagine how a friend or someone you admire might be in the situation and try to 'act cool' like them.

Sometimes you have to 'give to get'! Without forgetting about what you want, try to find a way of meeting the other person half-way. See if there is something else you can offer whilst keeping hold of your 'no'. Maybe reduce your demand to something that can be fulfilled.

Turn the problem over to the other person! Ask them for what you can do together, but without giving in to something you are not happy with. E.g. say, 'I can't say yes to that, even though you want me to . . . What can we do about it?'

How do you become assertive?

Being assertive is not always easy . . . The best way to build your confidence is through *practice!!*

Can you think of any situations in your day-to-day life where you could practise being assertive? Remember it might be easier to start small!

Here are some examples if nothing comes to mind straight away . . .

- Go to a shop and ask where something is (e.g. in a chemist's, ask for the shampoo).
- While talking with someone, change the subject to something you want to talk about.
- Ask for no sauce/a different topping in a fast-food restaurant.
- Ring directory enquiries for a phone number.
- Ring the local swimming pool and ask for opening times.
- Invite a friend out to the cinema/shopping.
- Go into a shop and ask for change for the bus.
- Ask a friend to do you a favour.
- Disagree with someone's opinion (e.g. say that you don't like *Eastenders*).
- Give someone a compliment/accept a compliment by saying thank you.

What happened when Cassie used an assertive strategy

'My friend wanted me to bunk off English with her as she hadn't done her homework. I knew she was really worried about it and I didn't want to let her down, but at the same time English is my favourite lesson! It's the only one I really enjoy at the moment, as we are writing poetry, and I really didn't want to miss it. She said I was selfish if I went to the lesson, as then she would have to go too. I decided to try being a "broken record". I told her I knew she was worried about her homework but I wasn't going to bunk off the lesson with her. She tried really hard to convince me but I just kept saying, "No. I like English. I'm not bunking off." I felt stronger every time I said it! After a while she accepted it and we talked about what excuses she could give for not doing her homework.'

Situation/s I will practise being assertive in

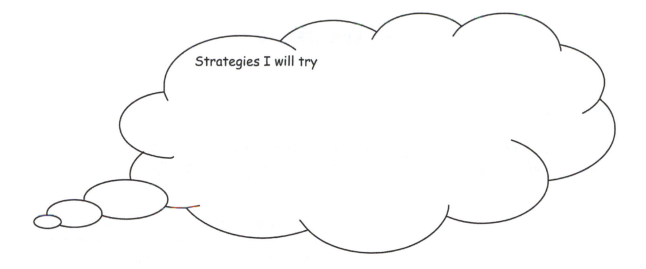

Strategies I will try

How I got on

'BEST skill'

Guidelines for achieving your objectives effectively: getting what you want (as long as it's reasonable!)

B
e clear

E
xpress your feelings

S
ay what you want

T
ry to negotiate

- **Be clear** when explaining the situation you are in. Stick to the facts and give the person a clear description of events or experiences you need to talk about. Do not include judgements or assumptions of the other person's motives.
- **Express your feelings.** Give a brief non-blaming description of any feeling triggered by the situation. Start the sentence with 'I feel . . .' or 'This makes me feel . . .' rather than 'You make me feel . . .'
- **Say what you want** in a confident and clear way, holding strong in your position and ignoring threats. Ask for changes in behaviour, not attitude, personality or beliefs. Only ask for one change at a time and something that can be changed now. Be specific. If they are happy to do what you want, stop here. If not, try to negotiate.
- **Try to negotiate:**
  - Turn the tables by turning the problem over to the other person by asking them for alternative solutions, e.g., 'What do you think we should do?' or 'How can we solve this problem?'
  - Be willing to give and get. Stick with 'no' but offer to do something else to solve the problem another way. Focus on what will work.
  - Motivate the other person with a reward by explaining the consequences. Tell the person the positive effects of getting what you want or need. Help the person feel good ahead of time for doing or accepting what you want. Reward him/her afterwards.
- Good negotiation skills are very effective and useful in helping us to get what we want.

WORKSHEET 40

'My anger scale'

10

9

8

7

6

5

4

3

2

1

WORKSHEET 41

'Help with challenging your thoughts'

Sometimes the words that you use to describe yourself are also self-critical thoughts!
Write any of your self-critical thoughts in the box below:

Think back to when you worked on challenging your thoughts . . .
Use Worksheet 30 'Help with challenging yourself' to check them out and find
alternatives . . .

Choose three alternative thoughts that challenge your critical thoughts about
yourself or positive words from the previous exercise and write them in the left-
hand boxes . . .

Over the next week
look for the evidence
to support your new
thought . . .

It might be something
you do, or something
someone tells you . . .

Write your evidence
in the boxes on the
right . . .

Self-critical thoughts

Unlovable . . . Moody . . . Fat . . .

Jessica looked back at her thought record and saw her previous evidence for and against her NATs. She wrote down the alternatives and went to look for evidence during the week . . . .

*Sometimes I get moody, but so does everyone . . . and I'm happy a lot of the time . . . It's good that I can show my feelings . . .

*When I feel bad that I'm moody I should just check out if that's how I really come across . . .

*My mate Sonia said she wishes she could be more like me and let people know she felt crap and didn't feel like mucking around that day . . .

*My support worker said what a good week I had had and how lovely it was to be around me . . . But I had thought I had been a right moody cow . . .

'Facing my fears ladder'

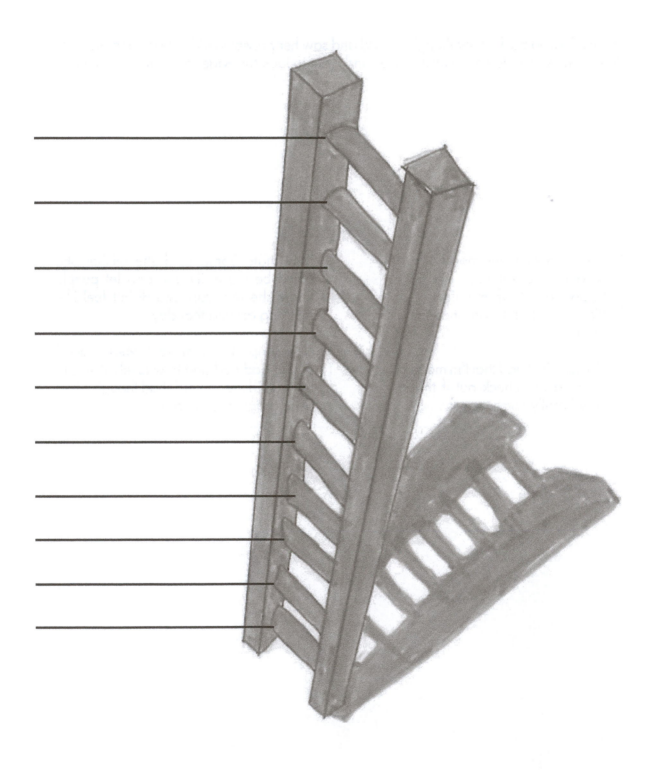

'Riding the wave'

When it seems as though what you are feeling is going to wash you away in a tidal wave . . .

Just stay with it . . .

Remember the feeling will not stay this intense for ever.

It *WILL* pass . . .

You just need to ride it out!

So go on!! Get on your surfboard and ride the wave!

What do I need to help me surf the wave?

WORKSHEET 44

'Mindfulness'

Taken from Linehan 1993

Previously we've looked at the range of different feelings we experience, and talked about how, even though sometimes we think we shouldn't feel certain things, our feelings can often be helpful.

Mindfulness means paying attention in a particular way: on purpose, in the present moment, and non-judgementally. This can mean being aware of and accepting your thoughts and feelings without trying to stop them.

We have different ways of seeing things and behaving, depending on what frame of mind we are in. One way of looking at these different minds is to divide them into three:

our '**Wise Mind**', our '**Emotional Mind**' and our '**Reasonable Mind**'.

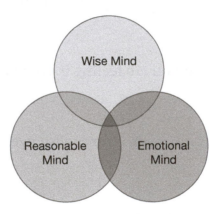

When we are in our '**Emotional Mind**' we are led by our feelings! It is almost impossible to think about things reasonably because we act based on our feelings and we may overreact to things . . . This is when you 'can't think straight'.

When we are in our '**Reasonable Mind**' we are able to think in a logical way. We approach things in a cool, non-emotional way (e.g. revising for something). This is when you are 'thinking straight'.

When we are in our '**Wise Mind**' we have the benefit of both our Reasonable Mind and our Emotional Mind, plus 'gut feeling'! So we are able to recognise our feelings and think rationally . . . You can feel and think straight and have a feeling of what is the best decision for you, which helps you make more helpful decisions about what to do and how to feel better (e.g. ride the wave, self-soothe or distract, etc).

Being mindful is about balancing our **Reasonable Mind** and **Emotional Mind** to achieve a **Wise Mind**. We need feelings, but we don't want them to take over! If intense feeling occurs, suspect Emotional Mind. Give it time; if you are still certain about something, especially when you are feeling calm and secure, suspect Wise Mind.

 Mark is in his bedroom alone. He has had a really bad day and an argument with his dad. He feels angry and depressed inside. He is listening to depressing hard rock music and he is getting his razor ready to cut his arm.

 Which mind do you think Mark is in?

 Mark starts to think about the argument with his dad. He pieces it together a bit and begins to see how the argument developed out of nothing.

 Which mind do you think Mark is in now?

Imagine that Mark is able to go into his Wise Mind . . . What might happen?

 Mark recognises he is feeling angry and depressed and he is able to see how the argument and the bad day at school led to him feeling this way. He's now in a position to make a decision about what to do next . . .

WORKSHEET 45

'How to get into your wise mind'

Learning to be in control of your mind, not letting your mind be in control of you!

When you are in your **Wise Mind** you are aware of what is happening, how you feel, what you are thinking and experiencing. In order to get into your **Wise Mind** (and be able to make reasonable decisons when you get a surge of feelings) you have to notice what is going on right then in that moment. You almost need to press a 'pause button' and notice in detail all that you are experiencing, feeling and thinking. It is like you are stepping into yourself and observing everything that is going on without trying to change it.

Having a **Wise Mind** is easier when people feel good, and much harder when they don't.

STEP 1 – Observing

This is sensing or experiencing without describing or labelling the experience. It is noticing or paying attention to something.

> Consider in your head what is going on for you *right now*.
> Imagine this instant is freeze-framed.

Now the trick is to **stay** with the awareness, stay in your Wise Mind.

Naturally we try to stop painful feelings or only hold on to feelings that we like . . . Just try staying with your awareness without trying to change it.

Keys that might help:

Try not to judge what is going on for you. It is neither good nor bad. Just let it happen.

 Focus on one thing in the moment. If worries, thoughts or distractions pop into your head, let them float by and try to turn your attention back to the focus.

STEP 2 – Describing

This is using words to represent what you observe.

> After considering in your head what is going on for you *right now*, describe what is happening in as much detail as you can.

Home-task

These exercises are very difficult. Everyone has a Wise Mind but some people may experience it rarely or never, and no one is in their Wise Mind all the time. It takes a lot of practice!

Below are some suggestions for you to try.

> Over the next few days, see if you can get into your Wise Mind . . . Don't stop what you are doing; just notice how you are doing it and what you are feeling!! Stay with it . . . Just be mindful of what is happening for you . . .

OBSERVING

Experience your hand on a cool surface, e.g. table or chair.

Stroke just above your upper lip, then stop and notice how long it takes before you can't sense your upper lip any longer.

'Watch' in your mind the first two thoughts that come in.

Imagine that your mind is a conveyor belt, and that thoughts and/or feelings are coming down the belt. Put each thought and/or feeling in a box near the belt.

No matter what happens, 'step back' within yourself and observe.

Observe thoughts and label them as thoughts. Maybe put them into categories, e.g. thoughts about me, thoughts about others etc.

Eat your breakfast and just observe what sensations and feelings you experience.

Listen to music and observe what you think and feel.

DESCRIBING

Try to describe some situations and jot down whatever comes to mind. Use the examples above or some others of your own.

If you have an argument, try to be mindful and observe then jot down words to represent what you saw and felt happening.

If something fun is coming up, make a mental note to try to be mindful and later jot down your observations.

WORKSHEET 46

'Self-soothing'

Here are some ways of thinking about soothing yourself when you feel distressed . . .

Highlight the ones that you like and add your own.

Things you look at . . .

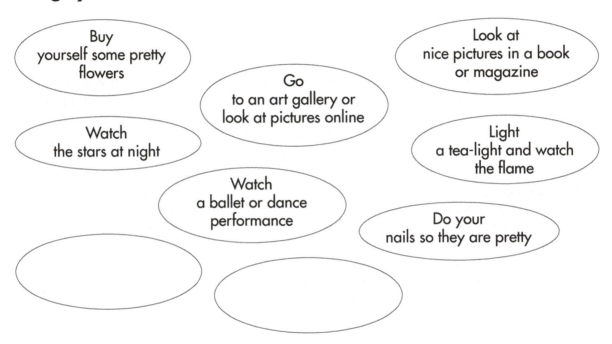

Buy yourself some pretty flowers

Go to an art gallery or look at pictures online

Look at nice pictures in a book or magazine

Watch the stars at night

Light a tea-light and watch the flame

Watch a ballet or dance performance

Do your nails so they are pretty

Things you listen to . . .

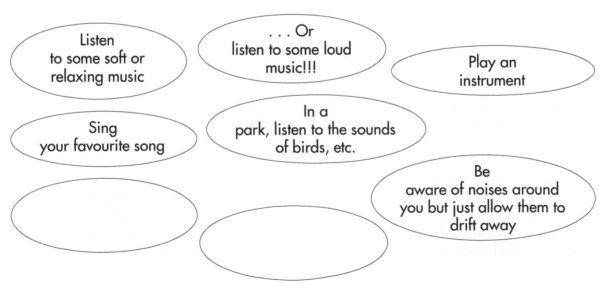

Listen to some soft or relaxing music

. . . Or listen to some loud music!!!

Play an instrument

Sing your favourite song

In a park, listen to the sounds of birds, etc.

Be aware of noises around you but just allow them to drift away

Things you smell . . .

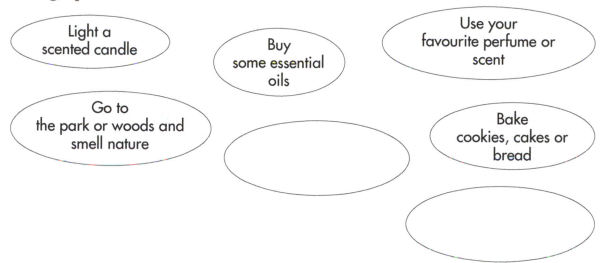

Light a
scented candle

Buy
some essential
oils

Use your
favourite perfume or
scent

Go to
the park or woods and
smell nature

Bake
cookies, cakes or
bread

Things you taste . . .

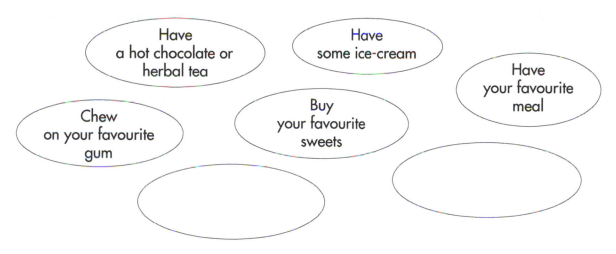

Have
a hot chocolate or
herbal tea

Have
some ice-cream

Have
your favourite
meal

Chew
on your favourite
gum

Buy
your favourite
sweets

Things you touch . . .

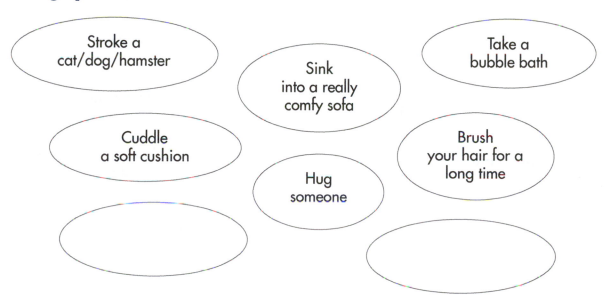

Stroke a
cat/dog/hamster

Sink
into a really
comfy sofa

Take a
bubble bath

Cuddle
a soft cushion

Hug
someone

Brush
your hair for a
long time

WORKSHEET 47

'What else can I do?'

Here are some suggestions of other things you can do rather than harming yourself. Read through them and tick the ones that have worked for you in the past, or those you would like to try . . .

Use a red, water-soluble pen to mark the skin instead of cutting	Make lots of noise! Scream, shout, bang a drum or pots and pans or cry
Write your negative thoughts on a piece of paper and put it in a safe place or rip it up	Write your thoughts and feelings in a diary
Give yourself permission not to injure yourself	Scribble on a big piece of paper with a red pen
Hold a chunk of ice against your skin or stick your hands in a sink filled with ice water	Put an elastic band around your wrist and flick it against your skin
Look at a picture of a previous cut	Eat something hot or strongly flavoured
Be aware of your surroundings – go through all five senses	Call a friend
Concentrate on your breathing. Use deep, cleansing, relaxing breaths	Watch a funny movie
Massage the area you want to hurt	Take a warm bubble bath or shower OR a cold shower
Look at photos/pictures	Throw beanbags

Read a book

Scream into a pillow

Build something with blocks or Lego and knock it down

Colour in a colouring book

Watch a video

Throw water balloons

Stay in a public place

Remind yourself that there are other ways to express and cope with overwhelming feelings

Play an instrument

Create and go to a safe/no injury place in your house/in your mind

Give yourself permission NOT to think of the memory right now

Rate your feeling on the feeling thermometer. Set your alarm for 15 minutes and at the end of this time re-rate. See if you still want to hurt yourself

Push against a wall/hug a big tree

Pet an animal

Take your pulse

Ask your therapist to make a tape with you that you can use during difficult times

Go for a walk in a familiar place or go for a brisk run

Clean up your room/change your room around

Write on a piece of paper that you want to hurt yourself and put it in a drawer. Leave the room and do something else for five minutes before coming back. Then, if you still want to harm yourself, write another message

Exercise.
Go Swimming

Write in the boxes the alternatives that have worked for you. You might have your own ideas, too . . .

'Sometimes I paint how I feel in my book. The pictures can be pretty gruesome but I don't show anyone – they're just for me.'

On you go!

WORKSHEET 48

'Staying safe'

Think about the future and write down a list of possible events, people's reactions, feelings and thoughts that would push you into harming yourself again.

1.

2.

3.

4.

5.

6.

7.

8.

9.

10.

11.

12.

13.

14.

15.

'My life plan'

What are your personal goals for the next week, month, etc.? Think of your goals in all the different areas of your life and try to fill in as many of the boxes as possible.

	Diet	Relationships/ friends	Hobbies	School/ college/ work	Lifestyle	Family
1 week						
1 month						
2–6 months						
6–12 months						
1–2 years						

'First-aid kit and toolbox'

First-aid kit for future crisis

Write in the empty spaces of the first-aid kit different things that will help you to cope when in crisis in the future.

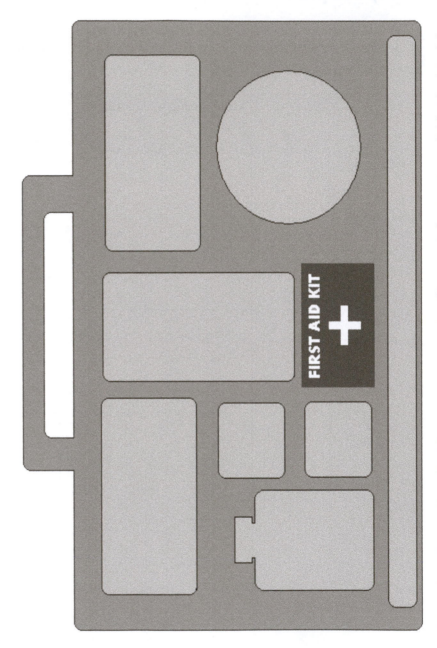

Keeping well toolbox

Write in the empty spaces of the toolbox the skills you will use in order to stay well.

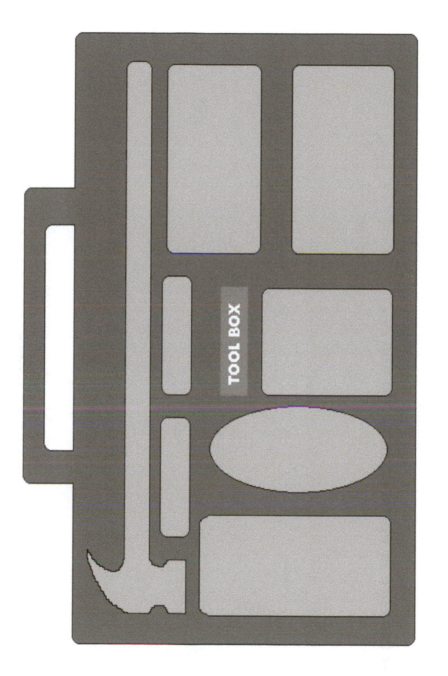

WORKSHEET 51

'My path'

Things I look forward to in the next 12 months . . .

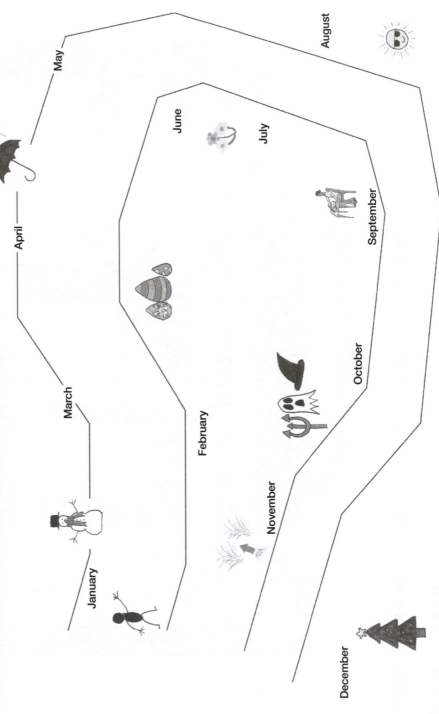

January
February
March
April
May
June
July
August
September
October
November
December

This is to certify that

_____

has successfully completed the CUTTING
DOWN programme!

Particular achievements include...

1. _____

2. _____

3. _____

Signed _____

Date _____

Index